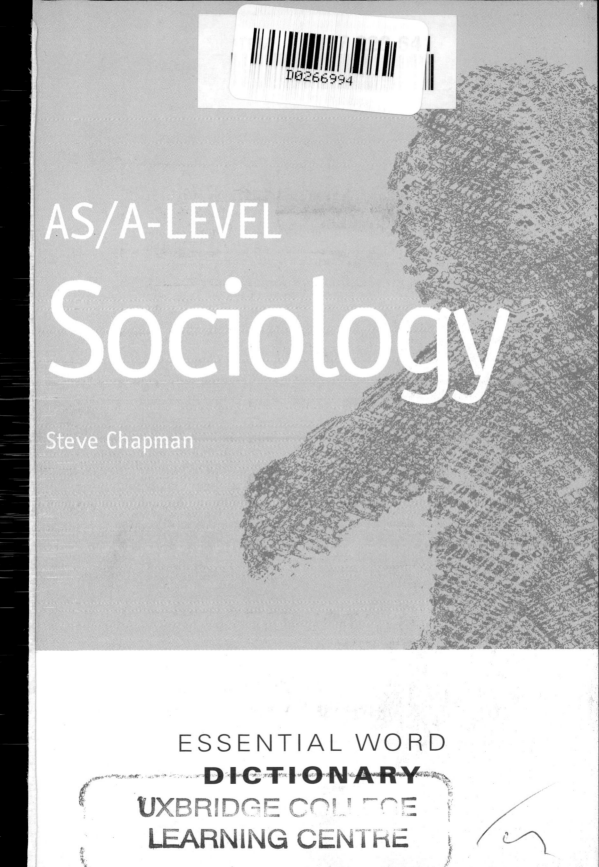

AS/A-LEVEL
Sociology

Steve Chapman

ESSENTIAL WORD
DICTIONARY

To Leyla for her support despite my tantrums and to my sons, Jake and Joe.

Philip Allan Updates
Market Place
Deddington
Oxfordshire
OX15 0SE

Tel: 01869 338652
Fax: 01869 337590
e-mail: sales@philipallan.co.uk
www.philipallan.co.uk

ISBN 0 86003 379 1

Acknowledgements

I would not have produced this dictionary without the long-term influence
of the following individuals. I would like to thank Hans Christian Day for
ruining what looked liked a perfectly interesting career in accountancy by
introducing me over a pint to the vagaries of sociological argument when
I was an impressionable young man. The late Steve Goodman inspired me
to become a teacher of sociology when accountancy was still an attractive
option, and my experience of the teaching of Bernard Wakefield confirmed
I had made the right decision.

P00024

Printed by Raithby, Lawrence & Co Ltd, Leicester

Introduction

In 1989 Anthony Giddens defined sociology as a dazzling and compelling exercise that aims to investigate our behaviour as social beings. He pointed out that the scope of sociology is extremely wide in that it ranges from the analysis of passing encounters between people in the street to the investigation of worldwide social processes such as globalisation. This dictionary aims to help you make sense of those wide-ranging social behaviours and processes. Most importantly, the purpose of this dictionary is to identify the most essential sociological terms and concepts in order to enhance your knowledge and understanding of those topics covered by the AS and A2 specifications for both AQA and OCR sociology.

There are many other sociology dictionaries on the shelves but on the whole these contain definitions above and beyond the needs of the A-level sociology teacher and student. This dictionary is deliberately slim because it includes only those terms and concepts judged to be the most relevant for exam success. It is therefore an essential tool for any AS and A2 student wanting concise and accessible definitions that can be used practically in an examination or coursework context.

In the dictionary, each word is broken down into a maximum of four parts or a minimum of one. Each entry begins with a single sentence definition. A second paragraph aims to elaborate on the definition. For example, it may refer to relevant sociological debates or specific studies which enhance your understanding of the term or concept. Third, if relevant, there may be an example of how the term or concept works in practice. Fourth, there is sometimes an examiner's tip. This may be a warning that the term or concept is commonly misunderstood or confused with another word. The tip may refer to how the term or concept should be used in sociological debate or its relative importance. Finally, throughout the dictionary, there are italicised cross-references to other words that you may need to refer to in order to understand an entry fully.

If you are embarking upon the A-level in sociology, it is important that you recognise, understand and are able to apply the terms and concepts used in this dictionary. Don't panic! This is not as onerous as it sounds. The likelihood is that your centre will only cover three, perhaps four, topic areas per year. The good news is that this dictionary covers them all.

absolute poverty: a state in which people lack the minimum resources required for health and working efficiency, such as food, water, clothing and shelter.

■ Rowntree found high levels of absolute poverty in York in 1899, although when the study was repeated in 1950 such poverty had almost disappeared. United Nations research suggests that over 800 million people live in a state of absolute poverty in *less developed countries*. This type of poverty is also known as subsistence poverty.

■ *TIP* It is important to be able to compare and contrast definitions and studies of absolute poverty with definitions and studies of *relative poverty*.

absolute rate of mobility: the proportion of individuals in a particular *social class* who either move upwards or downwards in the socioeconomic hierarchy.

■ Such mobility normally occurs because of changes in the economy, the expansion of free secondary and higher education to the masses and the decline in the birth rates of higher status groups.

■ *e.g.* The *Oxford mobility study* (1972) found that a large proportion of the *working class* experienced upward mobility into *middle-class* jobs in the 1950s and 1960s. This was the result of increased demand for professionals and bureaucrats in the postwar period and free secondary education, which meant that sections of the working class were increasingly qualified for such jobs.

achievement: the successful attainment of a task or *goal*, which in Western societies is usually formalised through examinations and qualifications.

■ Functionalist sociologists claim that the UK is a *meritocracy* because achievement rather than *ascription* is used to select and allocate individuals to their occupational *role* and *status*.

■ *e.g.* Functionalists argue that a crucial function of education in modern industrial societies is to socialise children into accepting the *value* of achievement.

■ *TIP* The debate between functionalism and Marxism in regard to achievement is central to an understanding of the role and function of education.

action theory: see *interpretive sociology*.

administrative criminology: the view that most crime is opportunistic and committed by young males because the benefits of crime outweigh the risk and cost of being caught.

a

■ Administrative criminologists such as Mayhew would tackle crime by making sure the potential costs of crime always outweigh the benefits by either increasing the risk of being caught or making sure there are fewer opportunities for crime through *target-hardening*.

■ *e.g.* Anti-crime policies such as 'three strikes and you're out' and *zero tolerance* are admired by supporters of this view.

■ *TIP* This view is central to debates about social control and social policy solutions to crime.

affective relationships: relationships that are primarily defined by emotion, e.g. those based on love or close family connections.

affirmative action: a type of *positive discrimination* practised in the USA, mainly aimed at increasing the number of African-Americans in key employment sectors such as the military, the police and professions, especially in management positions.

affluent worker study: a classic piece of sociological research carried out by John Goldthorpe and David Lockwood in the 1960s aimed at refuting the idea of *embourgeoisement*.

■ Goldthorpe and Lockwood's research demonstrated that the *working class* still retain a distinctive *class identity* in terms of values, politics and family life which distinguishes them from the *middle class*.

■ *TIP* The affluent worker study is now rather dated. More useful contemporary studies that cover much of the same ground include Marshall (1988) and Devine (1992).

African-Caribbean: a term used to refer to those members of the black minority ethnic group living in the UK whose origins can be traced to Caribbean islands such as Jamaica, Trinidad etc.

■ It is often used synonymously with the term 'West Indian'.

■ *TIP* It is useful to remember that the terms 'African-Caribbean' and 'West Indian' are problematic because they imply that this group shares a common culture. In reality, there are quite distinct cultural differences between people from different Caribbean islands.

ageism: *discrimination* based upon negative stereotypes, usually focusing on the elderly.

■ Ageist *stereotyping* suggests a strong connection between old age, sickness and disability and dependency.

■ *e.g.* Evidence of ageism can be seen in media representations of the elderly as dependent, helpless and miserable as well as the general media portrayal of teenagers as a social problem.

agenda-setting: the power of the mass media to decide which events or issues are most deserving of public attention.

■ Marxists suggest that those who own and control the media may use this power to exclude issues that are critical of the *establishment* or *capitalism*.

a

■ *e.g.* The *Glasgow University Media Group*'s research on the reporting of strikes in the early 1980s concluded that journalists set an agenda which was predominantly anti-union, pro-management and consequently supportive of capitalist interests.

■ *TIP* The concept of agenda-setting is part of a very complex and inconclusive debate about whether owners, editors, journalists, governments or audiences determine media content.

agents of social control: a term, mainly used by *critical sociologists*, to describe agencies such as the police, the courts, prisons, social workers, teachers etc.

■ These groups are seen as responsible for ensuring members of society conform to socially acceptable modes of behaviour.

■ *TIP* Marxists sometimes describe these agencies as 'agents of capitalism'.

age stratification: a system of inequalities that are the product of a society's positive or negative treatment of particular age-groups.

■ In Western societies age is not merely a biological state. The elderly and the young are also generally accorded a low social *status* because they are perceived as relatively socially incompetent.

■ *e.g.* In the UK, the elderly are often excluded from a number of areas of social life such as paid work when they reach 60–65, and consequently experience loss of *role* and status, isolation and loneliness.

■ *TIP* Don't make the mistake of treating the young and the elderly as homogeneous groups, because the experience of both the young and the elderly differs across *social class, gender* and *ethnicity.*

agribusiness: Western-based *multinational companies* that use industrial mass-farming techniques in *less developed countries* because they are cost effective and generate greater profits.

■ This type of production is seen by *critical sociologists* such as Gorz to be a problem in the developing world because the production of cash crops for export to the West monopolises fertile land that could be used for growing subsistence crops.

■ *e.g.* Ethiopia suffered famine in 1985 whilst exporting coffee and cut flowers to the West.

■ *TIP* Other sociologists have been concerned about the implications for public health of the farming methods employed by agribusiness in the West such as the development of genetically modified crops.

aid: refers to the flow of resources from the *developed world* to *less developed countries.*

■ It usually takes the form of capital, military hardware, medicines and expertise.

■ *e.g.* Bilateral aid flows from one government to another whilst multilateral aid refers to loans, usually with interest, from organisations such as the World Bank.

■ *TIP* *Modernisation theory* views aid as a crucial tool of development whilst *dependency theory* sees aid as a form of *neocolonialism* leading to less developed countries experiencing *debt dependency.*

alienation: the inability of individuals to identify with the work they do.

■ Marx argued that the way work is organised in *capitalist* societies (e.g. assembly-line production) denies most workers *work satisfaction*. They experience work as meaningless and the consequent frustration and powerlessness generated by this creates social problems as workers look for satisfaction elsewhere.

■ *e.g.* Some sociologists see rising *crime* rates, *domestic violence* and *strikes* as the product of alienation.

■ *TIP* If studying work and leisure, be able to compare Marx's definition of alienation with that of Robert Blauner.

altruism: working primarily for the good of others rather than yourself.

■ Functionalists argue that medical professionals work for altruistic reasons, i.e. for the public good, and consequently they deserve their high status and rewards.

■ *TIP* This view is challenged by Marxists who see doctors as agents of capitalist control and commentators such as Illich who sees doctors as responsible for causing much ill health in modern societies.

altruistic suicide: the view that some people kill themselves because they see society as more important than themselves and consequently are willing to sacrifice themselves for the greater good.

■ The idea originated with Emile Durkheim who argued that some individuals commit suicide because they are over-integrated into society.

■ *e.g.* Japanese kamikaze pilots in the Second World War.

American dream: a set of cultural attitudes associated with the United States which suggests that any individual, regardless of social and ethnic background, can be financially successful if they have the talent and if they work hard enough.

■ Merton claimed that many Americans wish to achieve the material goals set by the American dream but access to educational qualifications and jobs is denied to lower socioeconomic groups despite hard work and talent. Merton argued that the resulting frustration or *anomie* causes high levels of crime in modern capitalist societies.

■ *e.g.* Merton claimed that social groups, such as the working class and ethnic minorities, turn to crime, such as burglary, robbery and drug-dealing, because of the emphasis the American dream puts on materialism and financial success.

■ *TIP* Merton's analysis of the American dream is a major theory of crime in capitalist societies because it suggests criminals are merely conforming to dominant capitalist values.

anomic suicide: the view that some people kill themselves after experiencing severe disruption to their *norms* and *values*.

■ The idea originated with Emile Durkheim who argued that some individuals commit suicide because the regulatory factors which normally govern their lives are turned upside down.

■ *e.g.* The 80% increase in male suicide between 1983 and 1993 may be the result of normative confusion about masculine identity, i.e. the *crisis of masculinity*.

anomie: a breakdown in, absence of or confusion about the norms of a *society* which usually govern the behaviour of a social group or society.

■ Durkheim claims that such normlessness may result in individuals not knowing what is expected of them by society and therefore not knowing the difference between right and wrong.

■ *e.g.* Robert Merton's work on *deviance* suggests that anomie is experienced when people experience a gap between the goals set by society (e.g. material wealth) and the means of achieving those goals (e.g. education, jobs etc.).

■ *TIP* Anomie as a concept is worth knowing well because it proves useful as an analytical tool in helping to explain social change, especially in the fields of identity, crime, suicide and religion.

anti-positivism: the view that the interpretations or meanings human beings use to make sense of social interaction are more important than the influence of external social laws in understanding social behaviour.

■ *Anti-positivist* or *interpretive sociology* is a critique of the *positivist* view that human behaviour is determined by social forces beyond the control of society's members that can only be uncovered using scientific logic and methods such as the *social survey*.

■ *e.g.* Anti-positivists prefer research methods such as *unstructured interviews* and *observation*, because these uncover the meanings behind social action by studying everyday life or by letting those being studied speak for themselves.

■ *TIP* The positivist versus anti-positivist debate is over-stated and most sociologists today use either *triangulation* or *methodological pluralism*.

anti-school culture: see *counter-school culture*.

apartheid: a system of *stratification* found in South Africa between 1948 and 1994 which segregated people on the grounds of race.

■ The white minority used legislation to divide the non-white population into three groups: Bantu (black), Coloured (mixed) and Indian.

■ *e.g.* These groups were denied full citizenship in that they could not vote in parliamentary elections, they could not marry or have sex with a white person, and use of public facilities such as public transport, parks, swimming pools and toilets was segregated.

aristocracy: see *upper class* and the *establishment*.

ascribed status: in non-industrial societies, status is determined by *ascription*, i.e. determined by birth, rather than by *achievement* as in industrial societies.

■ This may mean that opportunities for *social mobility* are extremely limited for those groups ascribed low status.

■ *e.g.* In some *less developed countries*, females are ascribed low status because of *patriarchal* religion.

ascription: a system in which *status* and therefore occupational, family and political roles are determined by circumstances of birth and inheritance such as gender, age, ethnic group, religion, wealth etc.

■ Societies characterised by such a system are seen as *closed societies*, because movement between jobs and roles is usually not encouraged and may even be punished.

■ *e.g.* The Hindu *caste system* ascribes status and occupational roles on the basis of religious purity and is therefore a good example of ascription in practice.

■ *TIP* Ascription is still important in the UK because high status groups such as the royal family and aristocracy have inherited rather than achieved their social positions and roles.

Asian tiger: a South East Asian country that has successfully industrialised and experienced rapid economic growth during the 1980s and 1990s.

■ Asian tiger countries are often included by sociologists as part of a category called the *newly industrialising countries* in order to distinguish them from their poorer neighbours, classified as *less developed countries*.

■ *e.g.* South Korea, Taiwan, Singapore, Malaysia and Indonesia in particular have experienced great economic success and in some cases have invested in factories in the UK.

■ *TIP* Despite their economic development, be aware that some sociologists argue that these countries can still be classed as less developed than the West because their peoples experience greater extremes of rural and urban poverty than that experienced in the West and often lack basic political, social and human rights.

assimilation: the idea, commonly held in the 1950s, that racial harmony could be achieved by immigrants to the UK shedding their *ethnic minority* values and adopting the culture of the host population.

■ This idea neglected the persistence of white *racism* and underestimated the strength and vitality of ethnic minority cultures.

■ *TIP* The idea of assimilation has largely been abandoned in favour of *multi-culturalism*.

assisted places scheme: a type of educational scholarship set up in the 1980s as part of the 1980 Education Act to help bright children from working-class and low-income backgrounds to benefit from education at independent schools.

■ Studies of the scheme in the 1990s concluded that very few of the pupils who had benefited from the scheme came from working-class backgrounds. Most were the children of privately educated middle-class and professional lone parents, and especially the children of teachers.

■ *TIP* Despite the abolition of the policy in 1997, it is a good example to use to illustrate that education benefits some social groups at the expense of others.

attenuated extended family: a network of *nuclear families* who tend to be geographically dispersed but who feel attached by a sense of obligation to each other.

■ Physical contact between these families is probably infrequent because of distance, but they have symbolic contact on birthdays, at Christmas etc. and come together in times of family crisis such as funerals or family celebrations such as weddings.

audience studies: research that appeared in the 1990s that aims to explore how audiences receive and interpret media content.

■ This type of research is also known as reception analysis. It generally concludes that audiences, even those composed of children, are skilled readers of the media.

■ *e.g.* Buckingham's research into children and advertising concluded that children as young as 7 years old were capable of interpreting and rejecting advertising messages.

■ *TIP* Use this as a critique of *media effect* models which suggest that impressionable audiences are negatively influenced by media content.

authoritarian populism: a form of political leadership that is able to convince the general public that a strong political will and the full authority of the *state* are being used to address their concerns.

■ Stuart Hall used the concept to describe Thatcher's leadership style. She attracted popular admiration in the way she used the power of the state such as the law and the police to deal firmly with what the general public perceived as potential threats to their standard of living or social order such as the trade unions, crime and immigration.

authority: a form of *power* that is generally and widely accepted as legitimate.

■ Weber noted that authority could be rooted in traditions and customs and the charisma of a powerful personality (see charismatic authority). However, in modern states, *legal-rational* authority is the norm, i.e. authority based on the law and written rules.

■ *e.g.* Teachers and police officers derive their authority from these sources and consequently are able to enforce rules and *sanctions*, usually, although not always, with the agreement of the majority of society.

automation: a system of manufacture once characterised by assembly-line production and today characterised by computer-controlled technology, which has displaced rather than replaced human labour.

■ Marx was very sceptical about the benefits of automation, claiming it led to the greater control, *exploitation* and *alienation* of the workforce.

■ *e.g.* The *Marxist* Harry Braverman sees automation as assisting the *deskilling* of both the manual and non-manual workforce and claims it has led to the *proletarianisation* of *white-collar workers*.

autonomy: the power to choose one's own actions.

■ This concept is often used by *interpretivist sociologists* who are sceptical of the *positivist* belief that human actions are constrained by social forces beyond our control.

■ *e.g.* Interpretivists point out that human beings have consciousness and *free will* which they use to interpret the world around them. Consequently, people actively construct their own social reality rather than have it imposed upon them.

banding: a form of *streaming* or setting used in schools.

■ Studies of *classroom interaction* suggest differential treatment of bands by teachers may result in pupils internalising positive or negative self-esteem that may impact on educational performance.

■ *e.g.* There is some evidence that banding may result in school *counter-cultures* appearing amongst those pupils allocated to bottom bands.

■ *TIP* Marxists see banding as a means by which the *hidden curriculum* convinces working-class pupils that they are to blame for their own educational failure and therefore deserving of manual work.

bias: any situation in which the *reliability* of research methods and/or the *validity* of research findings are distorted.

■ Bias may be caused either by political or moral beliefs prejudicing the objectivity of the research or by problems in the research design.

■ *e.g.* A sociologist may select only those aspects of the research findings that fit his or her hypothesis or ideological position, or the research may be flawed because it is based upon a biased sample or research tool that 'leads' respondents into particular responses that support the sociologist's position.

■ *TIP* Sociologists such as Gomm, Phillips and Gouldner point out that it is impossible for sociology to be totally bias-free because it is a social activity carried out in a social world characterised by conflict between competing groups.

bilateral aid: see *aid*.

biological analogy: an analogy used by *functionalists* that suggests that society is similar to the human body because the social institutions which make up the social system are like internal organs working together to bring about *social order* in the same way that real organs function together to maintain health.

■ The main function of these institutions such as education, work, religion, law, the family etc. is to work together to maintain social equilibrium or order.

■ *e.g.* If any of these institutions breaks down or does not perform its function efficiently, functionalists believe that society will experience negative symptoms such as an increase in *social problems*.

biological determinism: a theory that emphasises biological or genetic causes for human behaviour, especially differences between males and females.

b

■ This theory particularly influenced the work of functionalist sociologists, such as Parsons and Murdock, whose work was based on the premise that femininity and masculinity are genetically determined and therefore gender roles are fixed and unchangeable. Feminists have challenged this argument and argued that biological differences cannot explain the social roles that societies attach to gender. They suggest that gender roles are socially constructed through *socialisation*.

biomechanical model of health: the approach to health care subscribed to by the medical profession which takes credit for the general decline in *mortality rates* and the increase in life expectancy experienced during the course of the twentieth century.

■ This model, also known as biomedicine, concentrates on the organic or physical symptoms of disease and portrays doctors as the only people who have the necessary skills to identify and treat these symptoms.

■ *e.g.* It stresses cure rather than prevention through drugs, surgery etc.

■ *TIP* Be aware that some sociologists such as McKeown, working from the perspective of the *social model of health*, claim that factors such as sanitation, improved nutrition and better standards of living are the main cause of better health today, whilst Marxists see the biomechanical model as a capitalist ideology because it rarely locates the causes of disease in the capitalist-industrial environment.

biomedicine: see *biomechanical model of health*.

births outside marriage: in the year 2000, 37% of babies were born outside of marriage.

■ The *New Right* suggest that the fact that births outside marriage have increased and that the UK has the highest rate of teenage pregnancy in Europe is a symptom of family breakdown and moral decline.

■ *e.g.* The media have supported such anxieties by creating *moral panics* around the subject of schoolgirl mothers.

■ *TIP* Be aware that available evidence contradicts the New Right argument, because most births outside marriage are to stable cohabiting couples who eventually marry, whilst teenagers only make up 3% of lone parents.

black: a term used to refer to people who belong to non-white *ethnic minority* groups.

■ The term is regarded as having limited usefulness as some ethnic minorities, particularly those from Asian backgrounds, object to being described as 'black'.

■ *TIP* Some sociologists note that such a description disguises the richness of Britain's multicultural character as well as underplaying social class and gender distinctions.

black British: a term used to describe people from non-white *ethnic minority* backgrounds who are born in the UK.

■ Some sociologists, notably Johal and Modood, have focused on how black-British people construct their ethnic and national identity.

■ *e.g.* Modood's (1997) survey of ethnic minority groups found that most of his second-generation sample thought of themselves as mostly, but not entirely, culturally and socially British. They didn't feel comfortable with a 'British' identity because they felt that the majority of white people did not see them as British.

black economy: see *informal economy*.

black feminism: a branch of feminism which argues that *liberal feminism*, *Marxist feminism* and *radical feminism* have largely ignored the role of ethnicity and culture in bringing about gender inequality.

■ It is suggested that black women experience inequality differently from white women, because their everyday experiences encompass *racism* as well as *patriarchy*.

Black Report: a government-sponsored report that appeared in 1980, identifying the chief cause of ill health amongst the working class as poverty.

■ It suggested that material factors were more important than cultural factors in explaining the relatively poor *morbidity rate* and *mortality rate* of the working class.

■ *e.g.* The report identified the main causes of working-class ill health as insufficient household income (leading to poor diet etc.), overcrowded and damp homes, smoking and drinking resulting from stress, worry and depression and the failure of the NHS to focus its spending on preventative medicine.

■ *TIP* The Black Report is useful as a criticism of both *cultural deprivation theory* and the *biomechanical model of health*.

blue-collar workers: a term, originating in the USA, used to describe those who do *manual work*, i.e. the *working class*.

bourgeoisie: a *Marxist* term used to describe the *capitalist* class, who monopolise the ownership of property, especially factories and land, and who, through the ownership of banks, control the flow of capital, i.e. *wealth* and income.

■ Marx argued that this class grows even wealthier through its *exploitation* of the *working class* by keeping their wages low instead of putting a fair value on their labour.

■ *TIP* Be aware that some sociologists, notably Dahrendorf and Saunders, argue that the bourgeoisie is no longer important because capital has been dispersed by wider share ownership and those who control big companies today, i.e. directors, executives and managers, are rarely the people who own them.

British Crime Survey: a *victim survey* conducted annually by a team of researchers at the Home Office based on approximately 15,000 households, selected from all over the country and designed to be as representative a sample as possible.

■ The survey data suggest that only one in four crimes are reported to the police and therefore the BCS concludes that *official statistics* underestimate the real level of crime in society. However, it also concludes that fear of crime is out of proportion to reality in that the average person is unlikely to be a regular victim of crime.

■ *TIP* Some sociologists such as Jock Young are critical of the BCS's findings because·they underestimate the risk of crime in the inner city and therefore the realistic fears that many inner-city dwellers have about crime.

bureaucracy: the most effective form of modern *organisation* according to Max Weber.

■ It is run by officials appointed on merit with distinct roles based on specialised knowledge who know their place in a hierarchy of *authority* and who follow impersonal and rational rules in the making of decisions.

■ *e.g.* Weber argued that this model was well suited to a range of profit-making, military, political and religious organisations.

■ *TIP* Be aware that some sociologists see bureaucracies as *dysfunctional*, i.e. as having negative consequences for individuals and societies.

Calvinism: a type of ascetic Protestant religion, associated with the work of John Calvin in the sixteenth century.

■ Max Weber saw the beliefs and practices of this religion as instrumental in encouraging the emergence of *capitalism* in Britain.

■ *e.g.* According to Weber, early capitalists made great profits, which were invested in the Industrial Revolution by adopting the Calvinist *Protestant work ethic*, which encouraged hard work, self-discipline, thrift and the avoidance of idleness and leisure.

■ *TIP* Do not make the common error of assuming that religion 'caused' capitalism. Weber saw it as a key factor but he also acknowledged other influences too.

canalisation: an aspect of *gender role socialisation* that involves parents channelling children's interests into toys and activities seen as normal for that sex.

■ Oakley notes that these types of gender reinforcements are extremely powerful and that by the age of five, most children have acquired a clear *gender identity*. They know what gender they belong to and have a clear idea of what constitutes appropriate behaviour for that gender.

capital: in general terms, any asset that can be turned into income or counted as wealth.

■ *Marxists* see capital as those assets making up the *means of production*, i.e. money for investment, land, factories, machines, raw materials etc. and the profits generated by the *exploitation* of the *labour power* of the working class.

capitalism: an economic system in which the production of goods is organised for profit and sold in a free market.

■ The *means of production* and wealth are privately owned by a capitalist class which hires the *labour power* of the working class in exchange for a wage. *Marxists* see capitalist societies as class societies characterised by conflict, because they claim that the wealth and power of the capitalist class derive from the *exploitation* of the working class.

care in the community: the process of shifting the long-term care of the elderly, disabled and mentally ill from the state to the community in the form of families, hostels and GPs.

▓ The process began in the 1960s in reaction to the belief that mental hospitals were *total institutions* in which patients experienced *institutionalisation*. Community care aimed to help the mentally ill retake their place in society. However, the programme was accelerated by the Conservative government in the 1980s and extended to the elderly and disabled for ideological reasons.

▓ *e.g.* The Thatcher government strongly believed in minimal state interference in the lives of individuals, cutting the costs of the *welfare state* and the *privatisation* of welfare services.

▓ *TIP* Community care programmes can be used to illustrate the *New Right* approach to the welfare state.

case study: a technique which involves an in-depth study of a single example of whatever the sociologist is interested in.

▓ The example studied could be a person, group, organisation, community, nation or event. Usually a case study will involve the sociologist using a variety of primary and secondary methods to build up a multifaceted picture.

▓ *e.g.* Paul Willis's *Learning to Labour* uses a range of primary and secondary research techniques to build up a case study of 12 working-class boys in a Midlands secondary school whereas Peter Townsend's survey of poverty contains case studies of particular families and their experience of *poverty.*

▓ *TIP* Case studies are a form of *methodological pluralism.*

caste system: a type of *stratification* system found in the Hindu religion that ranks individuals at birth in a hierarchical fashion according to their religious purity.

▓ Individuals occupy an *ascribed status* and occupational roles are fixed.

▓ *e.g.* It is generally impossible to experience any form of upward *social mobility* through education, jobs or marriage.

casualisation of the labour force: a strategy adopted by employers when demand for products rises, which involves the hiring of temporary part-time workers and/or subcontracting-out particular types of work such as cleaning, catering etc. rather than providing them in-house.

▓ These particular work practices have been associated with the *post-Fordist* organisation of production, which stresses the need for fewer full-time workers and for workforces to be more flexible than in the past.

▓ *e.g.* Some employers use 'zero-hours contracts', which mean employees have to be available for work but are only paid when the company needs them.

catharsis effect: an idea mainly associated with the *uses and gratifications theory* of the media which suggests that watching television or films at the cinema may have the positive effect of releasing pent-up energy, tension and aggression.

▓ *e.g.* Watching an exciting sports event or being on the edge of one's seat whilst watching an action thriller may channel the aggressive energy of young people into safe areas.

CCCS: see *Centre for Contemporary Cultural Studies.*

C

censorship: the banning, restricting and classifying of various types of expression, e.g. free speech, writing, films, television etc., as a result of political and religious beliefs or as a means of protecting vulnerable groups such as children.

■ Forms of censorship exist to varying degrees in most societies but are most likely to be found in their most extreme forms in *fundamentalist* societies, which feel threatened by non-traditional ideas. In the field of media sociology, supporters of the *hypodermic syringe approach* believe that more censorship of television and cinema is required to protect children from exposure to sex and violence and possible imitation.

■ *e.g.* Classification of films into U, PG, 12, 15 and 18 is a form of censorship.

census: a government survey, carried out every 10 years since 1801 (with the exception of 1941), which delivers a questionnaire to every household in the UK.

■ The census aims to provide information about the size of the population as well as aspects of social lifestyle including income, housing, family size, ownership of cars, telephones etc. Generally, census data are regarded as highly reliable, although they do suffer from some methodological problems.

■ *e.g.* The 1991 census results, despite a legal obligation to fill in the census form, were undermined by a 2% non-response rate, because some people avoided the questionnaire as part of a protest against being registered for the poll-tax. Moreover, the census results were thought to underestimate the ethnic minority population of the UK because of confusion about the ethnic categories used in the questionnaires. In 2001 people were asked to identify their religion in order to overcome this problem.

Centre for Contemporary Cultural Studies (CCCS): a department of the University of Birmingham that in the 1970s and 1980s was mainly associated with a Marxist analysis of *mass media, youth culture* and *Thatcherism*.

■ CCCS studies of mass media such as the work of Stuart Hall focused on how *moral panics* functioned to appeal to popular anxieties about crime and immigration and led to an increase in the law and order powers of the Thatcher government. CCCS studies of working-class youth culture such as the work of Jefferson and Hall and Phil Cohen etc. have focused on how subcultural style symbolically resists the cultural *hegemony* of the *ruling class*.

charismatic authority: power deriving from personality, speaking prowess or a belief that the person possesses supernatural abilities.

■ Weber saw this type of power as conferring *authority* on religious leaders, generals and politicians, a power derived purely on the basis of their followers believing they had exceptional abilities. He saw this power as short-lived as followers often grew disillusioned with such leaders in the long term.

■ *e.g.* Evidence suggests that some leaders of religious *sects* and *cults* are able to sustain their authority for greater periods of time than politicians. Sect leaders are seen as inspirational by their followers because they usually claim to be prophets who have exclusive access to the 'truth' whilst suggesting that conventional religions have lost their way.

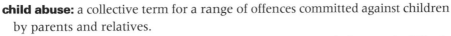

child abuse: a collective term for a range of offences committed against children by parents and relatives.

■ Such offences include neglect, physical abuse and sexual abuse. It is difficult to measure the true extent of child abuse. As Taylor notes, neglect and physical abuse are more likely to arouse suspicion than sexual abuse. *Radical psychiatrists* have suggested that 'emotional abuse' should be added to our understanding of child abuse. They point out that warring parents often use children as emotional weapons and this can psychologically damage children.

■ *TIP* The *reliability* of research methods such as victim surveys used to investigate child abuse and the *validity* of their findings have been called into question.

childhood: the period of biological and psychological development before adulthood which is also a social experience structured by strong cultural expectations in regard to the relationship between adults and children.

■ Some sociologists, notably Aries, suggest that childhood is a recent social invention in Western societies.

■ *e.g.* There is evidence that childhood in its present highly protected and controlled state in the West, with its associated paraphernalia of toys, games, books, laws etc., did not come about until the middle of the twentieth century and that this model does not exist in preindustrial and less developed societies.

■ *TIP* Experience of childhood is relative to experience of social class, gender and ethnicity.

Child Support Agency: a government agency set up in 1993 as a product of the Child Support Act (1991), which legally obliged fathers to provide financial support for children.

■ This agency does not merely collect maintenance from fathers who are separated or divorced from the mothers of their children. It also pursues fathers who have never lived with their children and who may deny paternity. The motives for setting up the agency were probably financial rather than the product of *familistic ideology*, because state benefits for single mothers are reduced on receipt of payments from fathers.

choice of research method: a decision that sociologists generally make on the basis of practical and ethical considerations rather than on the basis of where they stand theoretically (i.e. *positivist* or *interpretivist*).

■ *e.g.* Factors such as cost, monies available, access to the population being studied, size of research team, the nature of what is being studied, time available, the skills of the research team etc. are probably the important influences determining whether surveys, questionnaires, different types of interview and observation are used.

■ *TIP* A lot of studies, e.g. Willis, use *triangulation* for the practical reason that its use increases both the *reliability* and *validity* of the study.

church: an established religious organisation, usually in the Christian tradition, characterised by a formal and hierarchical bureaucracy of paid officials and which has a set of beliefs that is widely accepted.

C

■ Worship tends to be formal and ritualistic in its ceremonies. The church often has a formal connection to the *state*.

■ *e.g.* The Queen is the head of the Church of England and bishops sit in the House of Lords.

■ *TIP* Questions about religious *sects* often require reference to the concept of church.

city technology college (CTC): a type of secondary school set up by the Conservative government in the 1980s in reaction to the view that education was not producing the right type of scientific and technical skills necessary for economic growth.

■ CTCs were supposed to be set up and financed by a combination of government and local businesses in order to provide a science- and technology-based curriculum. However, to date, there are fewer than a dozen of these schools nationally and little private money has been forthcoming. Moreover, these schools have been criticised for their selective practices.

civil religion: events or activities that involve ritualistic patterns but generate the collective sentiments usually associated with religious ceremonies and occasions, such as a sense of belonging and solidarity.

■ Such events may exist on a personal level, e.g. registry office weddings, fervent support for a football team etc., or on a national level, e.g. *nation states* competing at the Olympics, Princess Diana's funeral.

■ *TIP* Note that civil religions are similar in character to *surrogate religions*.

class: see *social class*.

class boundaries debate: the arguments generated by the idea that the boundaries between the *working class* and *middle class* have disappeared as the significant difference between them, in terms of economic reward and conditions of employment, has declined.

■ Pahl (1988) suggests that the class structure looks like a diamond because the majority of the population belong to a 'middle-mass', with similar conditions and prospects. However, Abercrombie and Warde note that although the differences may not be as distinct as 50 years ago, classes can still be clearly seen with distinctive economic differences between them, although they may be blurred at the edges.

■ *TIP* The *proletarianisation* and *embourgeoisement* arguments have both contributed to the debate that class boundaries are disappearing or at least blurring.

class cleavage: see *partisan alignment*.

class conflict: a Marxist idea that focuses on the struggle between the *capitalist* class and *working class*.

■ Marxists insist that conflict between these classes is inevitable because the capitalist class exploits the working class by not paying them a wage which reflects the value of their *labour power*. The potential for class conflict is also inherent in the distribution of wealth and income, power, housing, educational achievement etc. However, Marxists note that class conflict is often reduced by the use of *ideology*.

■ *e.g.* The use of ideological apparatuses such as education and the mass media allegedly leads to the working class experiencing *false consciousness*.

class consciousness: a shared awareness held by members of a social stratum that they subscribe to a common set of conditions in regard to *market conditions*, relations with other social groups, especially those with more power and wealth, and life chances.

■ Marx argued that when members of the working class realised that they were being exploited by the capitalist class they would go from being a *class-in-itself* to a *class-for-itself*, and strive for revolutionary change. However, in the meantime the working class is experiencing *false consciousness*.

class-for-itself: Marxist term for a working class that is aware of its exploited position and that intends to overthrow the oppressive *bourgeoisie* through revolutionary means.

class fraction: the recognition that the main social classes are fragmented into competing and often conflicting internal groups or fractions.

■ The three main social classes — the capitalist class, middle class and working class — are not internally homogeneous. Rather they are composed of social groups that experience tremendous variation in pay, job security, and attitudes to education and lifestyle, and which compete against each other for scarce resources.

■ *e.g.* The working class is made up of those in secure employment and those who drift in and out of jobs. Skilled workers like miners often regard themselves as the labour aristocracy and consequently see themselves as having more status than other working-class occupations.

class fragmentation: see *class fractions*.

classical sociology: a term used to describe the sociology of the so-called 'founding fathers' of sociology — Comte, Marx, Weber and Durkheim.

class identity: the sense of identity and interest that derives from the type of work people do and their consequent recognition of their socioeconomic position relative to other occupational groups.

■ There is some evidence that the working class and upper class subscribe to a strong sense of class identity.

■ *e.g.* Many aspects of working-class lifestyle, especially political and trade union affiliation, are the product of a 'them versus us' identity that derives from poor relations between workers and managers in the workplace. Sociologists also note a strong sense of upper-class identity revolving around wealth, public schools, intermarriage, *cultural capital* etc. that results in distinct modes of language, mannerisms, attitudes and values that clearly distinguish them from the masses.

■ *TIP* Some *postmodernist* sociologists have argued that *consumption* has replaced class as the prime determinant of identity.

class-in-itself: a working class that is collectively unaware that its subordinate socioeconomic position is the result of *bourgeois* exploitation.

C

■ Such a class is seen by Marxists to be in a state of *false consciousness*.

■ *e.g.* Ruling-class *ideology* transmitted through institutions such as the educational system, the mass media etc. has convinced the class-in-itself that they should be happy with their lot.

class polarisation: the tendency for both the capitalist class and the working class to become aware of their differences and to become conscious of conflict between them.

■ Marx believed that full *polarisation* of the class system would occur when all members of the working class realised the degree of their exploitation by the capitalist class.

classroom interaction: the daily interaction between teachers and pupils in the classroom that is alleged to have both positive and negative outcomes for pupils in terms of their success or failure.

■ *Symbolic interactionists*, using *labelling theory*, have particularly focused on the pupil–teacher relationship and concluded that teacher expectations based upon stereotypical assumptions about social class, gender, ethnicity and behaviour may influence the self-esteem of pupils.

■ *e.g.* Some sociologists have suggested that teacher labelling of pupils can result in a *self-fulfilling prophecy* in that processes which evolve from labelling, such as *banding* or streaming, can result in the formation of *counter-school cultures*.

■ *TIP* Be aware that explanations which focus on classroom interaction have made a major contribution to our understanding of class, gender and ethnic inequalities in educational achievement.

class struggle: a Marxist idea which refers to any political and industrial action that is motivated by shared class interests and which aims to make the working class aware of its allegedly exploited status.

clear-up rates: the percentage of crimes 'solved' or cleared up by police forces.

■ Police clear-up rates vary according to the nature of the crime. The majority of violent crimes are cleared up, but the police record in regard to property crime is poor. This may reduce the reporting of that type of crime.

■ *e.g.* If members of the general public can see that police clear-up of burglary is very low (approximately 20%), they may fail to report such crimes.

closed/closed-ended question: the most common type of question found in *questionnaires*, which gives respondents a choice of answers that are usually pre-coded in order to assist quantification.

closed society: a type of society characterised by a *stratification* system that stresses *ascription*, fixed and unchangeable social roles and in which *social mobility* is not possible.

■ *e.g. Caste, feudal* and *apartheid* societies are examples of closed societies.

cluster sampling: a type of sampling that selects from a *survey population* that is divided into groups or clusters rather than randomly selected from the whole population.

■ A village, town or city may be chosen to be representative of a wider area.

- **e.g.** A sociologist may select a city and randomly sample a particular district, street, factory, occupation, school etc. depending on his or her research interest.
- **TIP** Cluster sampling is often used when a straightforward *sampling frame* is unavailable to the sociologist. In this case a map can act as an alternative type of sampling frame.

coca-colonisation: the process by which Western *multinational companies* (MNCs) increase their markets in *less developed countries* by persuading local populations that their wants or needs should be defined by the consumer culture of the West.

- Illich notes how people in less developed countries aspire to *false needs* because of intensive advertising by MNCs.
- **e.g.** Thirst may be translated into the need for a Coke, as people are persuaded that 'Coke is good for you' because it is a symbol of Western material success.

coercion: refers to rule by violence or the threat of force to achieve a social or political goal.

- Althusser notes that some governments use *repressive state apparatuses* such as the military, secret police etc. to control their populations, but these are not successful strategies in the long term because they create resentment. Althusser sees *ideological state apparatuses* as a more effective alternative to force and violence.

cohabitation: the arrangement in which couples, who are not legally married, live together as husband and wife, often with their natural children.

- Cohabitation has become more popular in the UK in the past 20 years.
- **e.g.** Cohabitation is most common among widowed, divorced or separated couples, although it is popular too amongst young couples. Recently sociologists have documented the rise in single-sex couple cohabitation.
- **TIP** Cohabitation is seen by the *New Right* as a symptom of the decline of the family, marriage and morality, although sociologists generally agree that cohabitation is a postponement of marriage, i.e. a prelude to it rather than an alternative to it.

collective bargaining: the official negotiations that take place between employers and employees represented by *trade unions* about wages, terms of conditions etc.

- Some Marxist sociologists see collective bargaining as the institutionalisation of class conflict — they argue that collective bargaining symbolises the channelling of potential *class struggle* into safe and manageable areas by the *capitalist* class.
- **e.g.** Members of the *working class* may believe themselves to be getting a 'good deal' in terms of the standard of living derived from collective bargaining and are therefore less likely to be in conflict with the capitalist system.

collective conscience: a term associated with Emile Durkheim and the *functionalist* theory of society, which refers to the shared beliefs, values and moral attitudes held by a particular society that are essential to *social order*.

C

■ Durkheim saw the collective conscience as extremely influential in *preindustrial societies* in which religion was central to the construction of a moral community and therefore to *social solidarity*. However, in industrial societies, in which religion is less powerful, the collective conscience is less important in bringing about social solidarity than the complex *division of labour*, which shapes order through interdependence of skills.

colonialism: the establishment of control and domination of territories and peoples mainly in the developing world by Western industrialised nations, largely by military means in the eighteenth and nineteenth centuries.

■ Colonial domination led to the enforced exploitation of *third world* labour, the transformation of third world economies to meet the needs of Western industry (e.g. the production of cash crops) and the imposition of Western social, economic and cultural values.

■ *TIP* Some *modernisation theorists* believe that colonialism has actually assisted the development of these nations post-independence, although the Marxist-influenced *dependency theory* argues that colonialism and *neocolonialism* are responsible for the *underdevelopment* of these nations today.

colonisation: the process by which some *working-class* values and political beliefs may have become part of the belief systems of some sections of the *middle class*.

■ The *Oxford mobility study* shows that in the postwar period a portion of the working class was upwardly mobile into white-collar and professional jobs, especially as the state sector, e.g. the civil service, education, health etc., expanded.

■ *TIP* Colonisation may account for why a significant proportion of the middle class vote for the Labour Party.

commodification: the process by which capitalism converts all aspects of life into 'things' or commodities to be bought, sold and consumed.

■ Sociologists have noted the tendency towards the commodification of health care, education, culture etc.

commodity form of incorporation: a term, associated with Dick Hebdige and his work on *youth culture*, that refers to the ability of the capitalist system to neutralise symbols of resistance found in deviant youth subcultures by turning them into marketable fashion commodities.

■ Hebdige notes that many of the more rebellious symbols of the punk youth culture in the late 1970s, e.g. body-piercing, ripped T-shirts and even punk music itself, were turned into fashionable consumer commodities available to the masses, thus reducing their shock value.

commonsense knowledge: the routine knowledge we have of our everyday world that generally guides our everyday activities and behaviour.

■ Our stock of commonsense knowledge is generally acquired through *socialisation* and is used to help us interpret each social situation we are in and determine the appropriate behaviour we should adopt.

■ *e.g.* Durkheim saw commonsense knowledge as riddled with prejudices and argued that only sociological knowledge could scientifically explain how societies functioned. Marxists, on the other hand, believe that commonsense knowledge is largely *ideological* and prevents exploited groups from achieving a true understanding of their position.

commune: self-contained and self-supporting group of families or individuals living and often working together, in which all members share property, living accommodation, childcare and communal duties such as household tasks.

■ Communes may be the result of religious, political or utopian ideals. They tend to be short-lived as individual self-interest tends to conflict with the collective sentiments of the group, especially as regards personal and/or sexual relationships.

communism: a political theory, associated with Marx, which argues that human societies can be organised in an *egalitarian* or equal way so that the *means of production* and therefore wealth are the common property of all and separate conflicting classes do not exist.

■ Until the period 1989–91 the term 'communism' was used to refer to the political ideologies of the USSR and Eastern Europe. Today it applies to China, Cuba etc. and is associated with a lack of democracy, centralised state control and human rights abuses.

■ *TIP* There is a notable gap between Marx's utopian ideals and the reality of communist regimes, which some sociologists therefore prefer to call 'state-capitalist' or 'state-socialist' government.

community (1): shared social relationships that are geographically based in areas or neighbourhoods.

■ There is a body of opinion that suggests that industrial urban society has undergone a *loss of community* and this is spreading to rural areas.

community (2): groups of people who share values, ideas, interests and lifestyles but who may not share geographical residence.

■ Recent sociological research has focused on the concept of *proto-communities* and the relationship between *nation states*, *globalisation* and *community*.

■ *TIP* Discussion of the concept of 'community' should go beyond physical communities to consider 'symbolic' communities.

community care: see *care in the community*.

community studies: a type of longitudinal method that involves a researcher or research team using a wide variety of *ethnographic* as well as survey-based research methods to study a whole community such as villages or small towns.

■ The wide variety of methods will include actually living among the community being studied and using *questionnaires*, *participant observation*, *structured* and *unstructured interviews*.

■ *e.g.* Young and Wilmott's (1957) study of family and kinship in East London is a type of community study, although the data were mainly collected through a social survey. Stacey's (1975) study of Banbury is another example of a quantitative-based community study.

C

■ *TIP* Community studies are good early examples of *triangulation* and *methodological pluralism* in practice.

comparative method: a research method, mainly but not exclusively used in *classical sociology* by Durkheim, Weber and others. It involves collecting data about a range of societies and social situations and comparing them with each other in order to identify variations and their causes.

■ Durkheim compared *suicide rates* of various societies and came to the conclusion that their constancy meant that suicide was the product of the social organisation of societies. He then compared the social characteristics of societies in order to find the common cause of suicide. Weber's work on religion used the historical method which is a variation on the comparative method.

■ *e.g.* In *world sociology,* Rostow's five stages of economic growth theory is a modern example of the comparative method in that he compares the social and economic conditions of developing societies with his *ideal type* and allocates them accordingly to different stages of development.

compensatory education: a type of educational policy, mainly found in the 1960s and 1970s, which involved the allocation of extra educational help and spending to inner-city schools with high proportions of working-class children and children from ethnic minorities.

■ This policy is a form of positive discrimination and was very influenced by *cultural deprivation theory*, which argued that the educational disadvantage of the working class and ethnic minorities was a result of deficiencies in their culture. Compensatory education was not a success. Some sociologists put this down to not enough money being spent on it. Others blamed the flawed theory on which it was based, whilst Marxists claimed compensatory education could not compensate for inequalities in wider society such as poverty.

■ *e.g.* The 1960s programme saw education priority areas in the UK and Operation Headstart in the USA.

■ *TIP* A contemporary form of compensatory education can be seen in the Labour government's introduction of education action zones in 1999.

competition: a key value of *meritocratic* societies such as those characterised by *capitalist* modes of production.

■ Functionalists see competition as a crucial value in the production and maintenance of a motivated workforce. They argue that competition results in the most talented and efficient workers rising to the top. It also keeps the workforce motivated because it provides the opportunity for people to better themselves.

■ *e.g.* Functionalists see the educational system as encouraging competition through social mechanisms such as examinations, qualifications, sports, awards, streaming etc.

comprehensive school: a secondary school that educates all children regardless of ability, social class, gender and ethnicity together under one roof. The schools were introduced from 1965 onwards as a response to the belief that the selective *tripartite system* of education was not *meritocratic*.

■ Comprehensive education has provoked a debate about standards in education with some critics suggesting that comprehensive schools are inferior to *grammar schools* and *private schools* in a variety of ways. Recent debate has focused on the possibility of reintroducing selection in comprehensive schools.

■ *TIP* Be aware that comprehensive schools may no longer be truly comprehensive because of *streaming* and catchment areas. They also exist alongside a diversity of secondary types of education including grammar school, *secondary modern school, city technical college* etc.

concentration of ownership: the transformation of British industry from a system of predominantly small competing firms to a concentrated structure dominated by large and monopolistic corporations.

■ Marxists argue that the concentration of ownership of British industry has consolidated the power of the capitalist class to exploit labour and impose its cultural values on society.

■ *e.g.* There is an important sociological debate about the ownership of media such as television and newspapers, which have become increasingly concentrated in the hands of companies owned and controlled by individuals. There are concerns about the influence of such ownership on media content and consequently the media's power to manipulate audiences.

concept: a term that allows sociologists to analyse, classify and give meaning to social phenomena and which forms the basis of social research.

■ Sociology is an academic discipline that deals with concepts, and sociologists are mainly interested in how *society* functions. Concepts can be descriptive and/or evaluative. They are rarely objective and are often loaded with value judgements.

■ *e.g.* The concept of *patriarchy*, depending on your perspective, can be seen as a natural and acceptable state or as a means of exploitation and oppression.

conflict theory: a theoretical perspective, such as *Marxism* and *feminism*, which focuses on the idea that society is characterised by a conflict of interest between those who have access to wealth, power and life chances and those denied that access.

conformity: behaviour that follows the established *norms* and *values* of society, which is normally the product of *primary* and *secondary socialisation* and which is reinforced by agencies of *social control*.

■ Behaviour that lies outside shared norms and values is defined as deviance and may be punishable.

■ *TIP* Think about how conformity may be encouraged by such agencies as education via the *hidden curriculum* and the media via *moral panic.*

conglomerate: a business corporation that consists of different companies with diversified interests in a very wide range of products or services.

■ There has been concern about the unchecked growth of media conglomeration and consequently the power of owners to manipulate media content and possibly audiences. Mergers and take-overs have continued at a steady pace in the newspaper and magazine and television industries, whilst American film conglomerates have long controlled studios, distribution networks and cinema chains.

■ *e.g.* Rupert Murdoch's News Corporation is a good example of a media conglomerate with diverse interests in television, film, publishing and newspapers.

conjugal roles: the domestic and economic roles played by husband and wife in marriage but now often extended to include *cohabitation*.

consensus: agreement about *values* and *norms* that exist in societies, forming the basis of *social order* and stability.

consensus theory: a theoretical approach such as *functionalism* which focuses on the idea that modern Western societies are characterised by a fundamental agreement on key *values* which form the foundation of *social order* in such societies.

Conservatism: a political philosophy which is generally associated with slow and evolutionary change in society or which is concerned with preserving traditional institutions, relationships and rituals.

■ During the period 1979–92, Conservative philosophy was radically transformed by *Thatcherism* into a concern with free-market principles, self-help and minimal state interference. Such *New Right* ideas often form the basis of Conservative policies and practices in the UK today.

conspicuous consumption: the idea that some consumption of goods and services, e.g. designer goods, attaches *prestige* and *status* to the consumer.

■ This idea is particularly associated with *postmodernism*, which argues that the *consumption* of designer labels is now comparable with social class, gender and ethnicity as an important source of *identity* in the twenty-first century.

consumption: the ways in which individuals use goods and services. The subject has become a major focus of study especially for *postmodern* sociologists.

■ It is argued that postmodern consumers experience greater choice and diversity in the marketplace than previous generations. They are able to construct identities around consumption patterns.

■ *e.g.* If we want to project a sophisticated and exotic identity we can choose from a global mix of consumer goods and foods.

consumption cleavage: social division that internally divides the working class and that is organised around new patterns of *consumption*.

■ Saunders (1990) argues that consumption of housing and transport particularly divides the working class.

■ *e.g.* Those members of the working class living in council estates may subscribe to different values from those who own their own homes.

content analysis: a research method that involves the researcher identifying a set of categories and systematically counting how many times each category occurs within a given area of the media. The interpretation and meaning of language and images used in media texts is also involved.

■ This method has proved popular in studies of gender and racial *stereotyping* and of political bias in the media. However, in recent years it has been criticised because chosen categories may reflect the values of the researcher and there is a tendency among researchers to assume that media content somehow affects the audience, which is unproven.

■ *e.g.* Studies that have used content analysis include Lobban's analysis of children's reading books and the work of the *Glasgow University Media Group* on the news reporting of *industrial conflict* and the Falklands War.

contra-culture: a type of *subculture* that is antagonistic to wider society and aims to overthrow it or change it by revolutionary and/or violent means.

contradictory class location: a Marxist idea that attempts to account for those people who fall between the three classes of capitalist, workers and *petty bourgeoisie*.

■ Managers and supervisors are involved in managing capitalist enterprises yet are also employees of those enterprises. They consequently occupy a class location halfway between capitalists and workers.

■ *e.g.* According to the American Marxist Erik Olin Wright, people in contradictory class locations may be pulled into either the capitalist or the worker position. They are there to be won by either side.

control group: a group in an *experiment* that is matched to an experimental group in every possible way but is not subjected to the influence of the *independent variable* in which the scientist or sociologist is interested.

■ The setting up of a control group is a crucial part of an experiment's design because if the experimental group ends up differing significantly from the control group this may be evidence to support the *hypothesis* that the variable had a significant effect.

control theory: the view, associated with Hirschi, that most people do not commit crime because they have controls in their lives which mean that the costs of crime far outweigh the benefits of crime.

■ Hirschi's theory has strongly influenced *New Right* theories of crime. He argues that much criminality is opportunistic — people choose to commit crime by rationally weighing up the benefits against the risks and costs (getting caught and being punished).

■ *e.g.* As people get older, controls in their lives such as attachment to family (e.g. marriage and kids), commitment to a career, active involvement in a community, reputation, and belief in rules and discipline mean that the costs of being caught committing crime are too great. Therefore most people choose not to commit crime. However, certain groups, i.e. the young, the working class, the *underclass* etc. are less likely to have such controls in their lives and the benefits of crime clearly outweigh the risks of being caught and punished.

■ *TIP* This theory has had a great influence on the Labour government of 1997 — especially in its arguments that more surveillance and harsher punishments will increase the risks and costs of getting caught.

convergence theory: the idea, promoted by Kerr et al. (1962), that both capitalist and communist industrial societies ultimately develop along similar organisational lines in terms of management styles, bureaucratic structures and social class hierarchies.

■ However, comparisons between the economies of Britain, Sweden and Japan indicate substantial differences in organisation, ownership, concentration, profitability and growth.

■ *TIP* Note the influence of this theory on *modernisation theory* in world sociology which assumes that developing societies should be converging on the American model of industrial capitalism.

conversionist sect: a type of *sect*, identified by Bryan Wilson, that seeks actively to challenge *secularisation* through evangelical means.

core nation: a term used to describe an industrial capitalist nation.

■ Wallerstein (1974) argued that such nations dominate the *less developed countries* whose economies are on the periphery of the global economy.

coroner studies: Atkinson's work on coroners' courts challenged Durkheim's assertions that *suicide* rates are determined by the social organisation of particular societies.

■ Atkinson concluded that suicide statistics are the end product of a complex interaction between the victim, the coroner and the family of the deceased, rather than being the product of social forces.

■ *e.g.* Interviews with coroners and observation of inquests led him to conclude that both the reliability and the validity of *official statistics* on suicide strongly depend on how individual coroners interpret suicidal clues in the lives of the deceased.

corporate crime: criminal offences committed by large companies that directly profit the company rather than individuals and are thought to be substantially under-represented in *official statistics* on crime.

■ *e.g.* Misrepresentation of products, price-fixing, industrial espionage, breaches of health and safety regulations, pollution etc.

correlation: a regular relationship between two or more variables that can be measured. It may be positive or negative.

■ *e.g.* The number of free school dinners in an area may correlate with the degree of poverty and educational achievement at GCSE. Areas with high numbers of free school dinners may have a higher proportion of failing schools. This may suggest that poverty is a factor which influences educational achievement.

correspondence principle: the view held by the American Marxists Bowles and Gintis that the structure of social relationships at school corresponds to the structure of relationships at work.

■ Bowles and Gintis argue that this aspect of the *hidden curriculum* has the effect of preparing working-class children to accept without question routinised factory work.

■ *e.g.* Both pupils and workers are allegedly encouraged to accept authority and discipline without question, to gain satisfaction from extrinsic rewards rather than work itself, to accept that work will be generally tedious etc.

■ *TIP* Bowles and Gintis are, of course, drawing attention to the hidden curriculum — you should evaluate their theory by focusing on the over-determinism of this concept and its neglect of the concept of resistance.

counter-culture: a type of *subculture* that rejects mainstream society and creates its own separate and alternative culture.

■ *e.g.* Some hippies in the 1960s formed *communes* that adopted environmentally-friendly and self-sufficient lifestyles and consequently rejected the material-istic and competitive lifestyle of mainstream society.

counter-school culture: a deviant anti-school *subculture*.

■ These may be formed because pupils feel that they are not valued by the school or because they do not identify with the value system and goals of the school.

■ *e.g.* Albert Cohen argued that subcultures are formed because teachers deny working-class boys status in the form of praise and qualifications. Consequently anti-school activity functions as an alternative source of status. *Labelling theory* similarly suggests that subcultures are a reaction to negative *teacher expectations* and *streaming*. However, Paul Willis's research indicates that such subcultures may simply be a product of working-class culture as working-class boys come to realise that they want jobs that do not require qualifications.

■ *TIP* Subcultural theories may be useful, especially when linked to the *crisis of masculinity*, in explaining boys' educational *underachievement*.

covert participant observation: a type of unobtrusive observation that involves researchers immersing themselves totally in the culture and lifestyle of the group being studied without declaring their identity as sociologists.

■ Some sociologists suggest that this method suffers from ethical problems whilst others claim it is the most *reliable* way of gaining insight into the natural world of groups that would not normally cooperate with sociologists or officialdom.

■ *e.g.* Simon Holdaway's **Inside the British Police**, in which Holdaway, a working police officer, secretly observed his colleagues as part of his sociology degree.

crime: a type of *deviance* which involves breaking the law.

■ The theoretical study of crime is extensive, although theories of crime tend to fall into six broad categories.

(1) Theories that focus on how crime might be beneficial to society.

(2) Theories that blame crime on the *pathological* characteristics of particular individuals or social groups.

(3) Theories that blame the way society is organised.

(4) Theories that suggest most crime is opportunistic, i.e. meaning that it is not planned and can be carried out by anyone.

(5) Theories that focus on the interaction between the law and particular social groups.

(6) Theories that take a *realist* view of the crime problem.

criminal statistics: the means by which crime is officially measured, based on statistics collected by the Home Office relating to crimes reported by the public, crimes detected and cleared up by the police and crimes prosecuted by the courts.

▨ Generally criminal statistics are regarded by sociologists as unreliable in that they probably tell us more about the attitudes of the general public, police officers, magistrates and judges than they tell us about crime and criminals.

crisis of masculinity: the idea that men's perception of what a man is and how he ought to behave has been undermined by profound social and economic changes.

▨ Mac En Ghaill notes that the *socialisation* of working-class boys has traditionally stressed the importance of *masculinity*, especially relative to the perceived inferiority of women. Masculine power is seen to be primarily expressed through work, which accords men the status of breadwinner and head of the household. However, the decline of manufacturing and primary industries such as mining, unemployment and the favouring of women in the creation of new jobs mean that boys can no longer feel sure about their future role as men.

▨ *e.g.* In education, this confusion may lead working-class boys to conclude that qualifications are a waste of time. The future looks bleak and without purpose so they don't see the point in working hard and consequently *underachieve* in education.

▨ *TIP* Be aware that this argument has also been applied to other areas such as divorce, domestic violence, urban riots etc.

critical criminology: a *neo-Marxist* theory of crime that attempts to explain crime in terms of class inequality, allegedly generated by the capitalist system.

▨ Taylor, Walton and Young in the *new criminology* suggest that some crime, e.g. property crime, is a political reaction as people become aware that the organisation of capitalism is responsible for their exploited and subordinate status.

▨ *e.g.* Gilroy argues that some African-Caribbean crime is a political response to racism and police harassment.

critical sociology: any sociological theory which is critical of the social and economic organisation of capitalist society.

▨ It includes *Marxism* and its neo-Marxist offshoots, those theories influenced by Max Weber, *symbolic interactionism* and various forms of feminism.

critical theory: see *Frankfurt School.*

cross-class families: families in which the husband and wife are both working but their occupations are officially categorised into different social classes.

▨ Feminists are critical of those classifications of occupations that only focus on the male head of household. They argue that in cross-class families it is the female's job that defines the lifestyle and status of the family unit. However, the evidence from empirical studies of social class in support of this view is mixed.

cult: a type of religious group that is often regarded by sociologists and the media as synonymous with a *sect.*

■ There tends to be no general agreement on how to distinguish cults from sects, although both the media and sociological use of the term tends to be loaded with negative associations of madness and sexual exploitation. Some sociologists suggest cults involve following a philosophy or theory rather than joining a group, giving up a lifestyle and/or following a leader.

■ *e.g.* Audience cults such as those organised around astrology may provide individuals with a personal philosophy or advice whilst client cults such as spiritualism may provide customers with a service.

cultural capital: a concept introduced by Pierre Bourdieu (1977) which suggests that middle-class individuals who subscribe to the dominant culture are able to use it as a form of capital in the education system to ensure educational success.

■ Bourdieu argues that schools are not neutral institutions — their organisational structures and content are defined by the dominant culture.

■ *e.g.* The way pupils are expected to behave, speak and learn in the educational system is defined along middle-class lines. Consequently middle-class parents transmit various linguistic and cultural competencies to their children that put them at an educational advantage over their working-class peers at school.

cultural deprivation theory (1): the view, embodied in a range of studies, that working-class and some ethnic minority cultures are deficient in that they fail to motivate their children educationally and/or to equip them with the skills and values required for educational success.

■ It is suggested that both working-class and ethnic minority parents are less interested in their children's education than middle-class parents. Moreover working-class child-rearing practices are alleged to be less child-centred than those used by the middle class. Finally it is suggested that working-class and ethnic minority children may be handicapped by *linguistic deprivation*.

■ *e.g.* Working-class parents allegedly socialise their children into the values of fatalism and immediate gratification which are seen to hinder educational progress.

■ *TIP* Don't forget that this theory underpinned programmes of *compensatory education* despite its neglect of *material deprivation, classroom interaction* and the influence of inequalities in wider society arising out of class and racism.

cultural deprivation theory (2): an approach found in the sociology of health and illness which suggests that the lifestyle choices of the working class and some ethnic minorities are responsible for their high rates of ill health.

■ The theory focuses on factors such as smoking, alcohol consumption, poor diet and lack of take-up of NHS facilities. However, it is criticised for neglecting material deprivation and the influence of inequalities in wider society arising out of class and racism.

cultural determinism: the view, usually used as a counter to *biological determinism*, that human behaviour is the result of culture rather than biology.

■ It is suggested that the sheer variation of human behaviour from one culture to another, especially in regard to *masculine* and *feminine* behaviour, is evidence that cultural influences such as *socialisation* are more important than biological differences. However, in recent years sociologists have tended to favour the view that it is the interaction between culture and biology that is important.

cultural diversity: see *multiculturalism*.

cultural dopes: term used by critics of *positivist* theories who point out that human beings are able to choose the course of their own actions and therefore are not culturally duped into behaving in predetermined ways.

■ Theories such as functionalism and Marxism tend to see human beings as shaped by social forces beyond their control such as *value consensus* and *social class* respectively. People are allegedly moulded into model citizens or model workers. *Interpretivists* point out that people can actively resist such processes.

cultural effects theory: a theory of *media effects* which suggests that media content produces long-term effects on audiences by structuring their cultural preferences and attitudes.

■ Studies of media representations of race and gender claim that the media reinforce prejudicial stereotypes about black people and women. Studies of *moral panic* claim that they needlessly raise public anxiety and prejudice against powerless minority groups. Some Marxist sociologists suggest that *mass culture*, transmitted by the media, contributes to the *false consciousness* of the working class. However, all these views tend to treat audiences as *cultural dopes* and neglect the active role of the audience in selecting and interpreting media content, as seen in *reception analysis* studies.

cultural imperialism: the aggressive commercial promotion of Western culture and specifically American culture in both the developed and developing worlds.

■ Western media institutions and especially Hollywood are seen to be creating a global empire of ideas based on the assumption that American values are superior and should be adopted by non-Western cultures.

cultural pluralism: see *multiculturalism*.

cultural reproduction: the transmission from one generation to another through *primary* and *secondary socialisation* of the key values, beliefs and norms of the culture of a society.

■ Functionalists see this as a necessary pre-condition for ensuring the maintenance of social order. Marxists, on the other hand, suggest that it is the cultural values of the dominant class that are reproduced, especially in institutions such as education, ensuring the maintenance and legitimisation of class inequalities.

culture: the shared beliefs, values, norms, rituals, language, history, knowledge and social character that make up the way of life of a social group or society.

■ Most sociologists agree that culture is largely the result of nurture via *socialisation* rather than nature. However, there tends to be some disagreement among sociologists as to the merits of different forms that culture might take, especially with regard to *high*, *low*, *mass* and *popular culture*.

culture industry: a Marxist idea which states that culture has become something to be manufactured and sold, in order to make a profit, by media *conglomerates.*

■ Marxists argue that the culture industry aims to manipulate the tastes, wants and needs of the masses by promoting a *popular culture* which is bland, uncritical and dehumanising. Other sociologists have expressed concern about the Americanisation of popular culture.

culture of poverty: a theory which suggests that it is the values and culture of the poor themselves that cause their poverty.

■ It is claimed that the poor subscribe to a value system of fatalism and resignation and consequently fail to take advantage of available opportunities to improve themselves. Those values are passed on to their children during socialisation.

■ *TIP* This theory has a contemporary cousin in *New Right* concerns about the *underclass* and *welfare dependency.*

custom: established norms of behaviour within particular communities or societies that are usually marks of cultural distinctiveness.

■ *e.g.* Queuing is regarded as a distinctively British custom.

cycle of dependency: see *welfare dependency.*

cycle of deprivation: the idea that experience of poverty in one aspect of lifestyle can generate further poverty from which it is extremely difficult to escape.

■ Two competing perspectives on poverty have emerged from interpreting this cycle. The *pathological* version of this concept evolves from the *culture of poverty* thesis and claims such a situation is the result of inadequate *socialisation.* The other sees poverty as an unfortunate consequence of a vicious circle of *material deprivation* or poverty. Both versions note that the result of these situations is poor school achievement and therefore unemployment or poorly paid jobs in adulthood. The cycle starts again when their own children are born.

■ *TIP* Note how the pathological version resembles both *cultural deprivation theory* and *underclass* theory.

dark figure of crime: the amount of undiscovered or unreported crime, which calls into question the reliability of the *official statistics* on crime.

■ Victim surveys such as the *British Crime Surveys* and *self-report* studies indicate a significant amount of hidden crime that does not come to the attention of the authorities.

dark side of the family: the view that the family is not always a safe haven and that it can be extremely *dysfunctional* for some individuals.

■ *Feminist* critiques of the family have particularly focused on the family as a location for abuse and violence against women and children, whilst *radical psychiatrists* have focused on how families may be emotionally and psychologically damaging for some members.

death rate: see *mortality rate*.

debt dependency: the debt which results from interest on loans from the West may result in some *less developed countries* finding themselves pressurised into supporting Western interests in return for a reduction or cancellation of that debt.

■ Some less developed countries have been forced into accepting transnational investment, making internal political changes against their will and ensuring their support for Western strategic interests.

■ *e.g.* Kenya was rewarded with aid for providing US forces with port facilities during the Gulf War.

de-centring of class identity: the view that social class is no longer an important source of identity for the working class.

■ Lash and Urry argue that recession and unemployment have undermined traditional working-class communities and organisations such as trade unions. The workforce has divided into two broad components.

■ *e.g.* The 'core', composed of secure workers with good rates of pay and promotion opportunities, and the 'periphery', composed of part-time, temporary workers on short-term contracts. The entry of large numbers of women into the labour market from the 1980s onwards has added to this diversity.

decomposition of capital: see *managerial revolution*.

deferential voters: a term used mainly in the 1950s and 1960s to describe some working-class voters who seemed to vote against their class interests by voting Conservative.

■ It was suggested that such voters were mainly older and resident in rural areas. They subscribed to an exaggerated respect for hierarchy and therefore political leaders with high social status.

deferential workers: workers who live in small towns or rural communities dominated by small companies, who are likely to have close contact with their managers and employers and who do not live in large occupational communities.

■ These workers are likely to subscribe to traditional values and vote Conservative.

deferred gratification: the decision to postpone immediate economic and emotional satisfaction that might be generated by leaving education at 16 or 18 and earning a salary, in order to achieve the longer-term goal of a university degree.

■ Subscribing to such a value is seen by *cultural deprivation theory* as a virtue and an important explanation as to why middle-class children succeed in the education system.

delinquency: illegal 'antisocial' and disruptive behaviour associated with juveniles or young people aged under 21 years.

■ Studies *of juvenile delinquency* have tended to focus on the influence of peer groups by examining gangs, deviant youth *subcultures* and *counter-school cultures*. Moreover, most studies have focused on white working-class youth and consequently there has been a neglect of female and ethnic minority delinquency.

delinquent subculture: a youth group which is seen as subscribing to norms and values that are defined by mainstream society as criminal, anti-social or disruptive.

delinquescent subculture: a *counter-school culture* identified by Hargreaves which was the result of working-class boys being placed in the bottom streams and being denied status by teachers.

■ The boys substituted their own value system and awarded status to each other on the basis of disruptive and sometimes delinquent behaviour. This confirmed teachers' expectations about their behaviour and consequently led to a *self-fulfilling prophecy*.

demand characteristics: a reaction by those taking part in research that involves them searching for clues about how they should be behaving and therefore potentially undermining the validity of the research.

■ It results from the fact that research situations are social situations. Those taking part in research will have concerns and anxieties about the motives or goals of the research that may impact negatively on their responses to questionnaires and interviews.

■ *e.g.* They may be concerned about how the researcher views them and consequently adjust their behaviour so that it is no longer natural.

d

demography: the study of *population* and population movement including birth rates, *fertility rates, mortality rates* and *migration*.

▨ In *world sociology*, it is argued by some sociologists that rapid population growth is hindering development in *less developed countries*.

demonisation: the transformation of individuals and/or groups into *folk devils* to be feared by society through the sensationalist and exaggerated news reporting found in the early stages of a *moral panic*.

denomination: a type of religious organisation that accepts and is accepted by wider society and does not have any formal connection with the state.

▨ Worship in these organisations is less formal than a *church* and less dynamic than a *sect*. Many denominations have broken away from the established church.

▨ *e.g.* The Methodist and Baptist religions are denominations rather than churches because their beliefs, although popular, are not as universal as those of the Anglican Church. Both broke away from the Anglican Church in the belief that the Church of England was losing touch with the fundamentals of Christianity.

dependency culture: see *welfare dependency*.

dependency theory: a theory, mainly associated with the Marxist Andre Gunder Frank in the 1960s and 1970s, which argues that the underdevelopment of the *less developed countries* is the result of systematic *exploitation* by the modern developed world.

▨ Frank argues that Western wealth and industrial development were based on a super-accumulation of capital generated by slavery and *colonialism* which guaranteed cheap labour and raw materials. Moreover, the West continues to exploit less developed countries by encouraging their dependence on the West.

▨ *e.g.* This involves dominating world-trade terms, encouraging *debt dependency* and the exploitation of less developed countries by Western *multinational companies*.

▨ *TIP* Note that in the 1990s this theory came under sustained attack because it failed to explain the increasing diversity of experience of less developed countries and especially the rapid economic growth of some of these nations.

dependent variable: an effect or variation in behaviour brought about, usually in a research situation, by the manipulation of an *independent variable*.

▨ *e.g.* More sex education taught in schools may result in a decline in teenage pregnancies.

desacrilisation: an aspect of *secularisation* identified by Bryan Wilson in which sacred and supernatural modes of thinking are largely replaced by rational and scientific modes of thinking.

▨ People have allegedly grown disenchanted with faith in God and the search for spirituality. It is claimed that these have been largely superseded by the demand for the material comforts produced by science and technology.

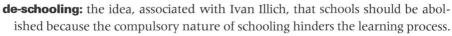

de-schooling: the idea, associated with Ivan Illich, that schools should be abolished because the compulsory nature of schooling hinders the learning process.

- Illich advocated a 'de-schooled society' in which an informal educational framework would exist in which people would volunteer to share their skills and resources with those who wished to learn.

deskilling: the process, identified by Harry Braverman, by which employers reduce the skills of their labour force in order to exert greater control over the production process.

- Deskilling involves management dictating how particular tasks should be carried out and consequently the worker is left with tedious and repetitive tasks. Braverman argues that the deskilling process is increasingly being imposed on *white-collar workers*.
- *TIP* Link this idea to the *class boundaries debate* and especially the concept of *proletarianisation*.

determinism: a concept subscribed to by *positivists* that suggests that people have no choice in their behaviour because their actions are shaped and constrained by social or biological forces beyond their control.

- *e.g.* Both functionalism and Marxism have been accused of determinism by *interpretivist sociology*.
- *TIP* Be able to contrast determinism with reference to *free will, resistance* and interpretivist sociology.

developed world: the economically developed capitalist world of Western Europe, North America, Japan and Australasia.

- It used to be known as the 'first world' and contrasted with the 'second world' (the communist countries such as the USSR, China etc.) and the 'third world' (the poorer countries of Asia and Africa). However, all these terms are now rather dated because of the collapse of communism in Europe and the economic success of countries such as the *Asian tigers*.
- *TIP* Instead of 'third world', the term *less developed countries* is more likely to be used by sociologists today.

development: generally this concept has been defined in a fairly narrow sense to refer to any industrial and economic development that results in rising living standards and more complex forms of social organisation.

- However, *world sociology* points out the problematical value-laden nature of the concept when it is adopted by theories such as *modernisation theory*, which equates development with Westernisation, or *dependency theory*, which equates development with socialism.
- *e.g.* Other sociologists point out that development implies progress, but some aspects of industrial development, such as environmental pollution, can be harmful. Others argue that our definition of development should be extended to include the concept of 'social development', i.e. the reduction in mortality rates, especially infant mortality rates, the increase in life expectancy, the eradication of poverty, the reduction in illiteracy and access to jobs.

d

deviance/deviant: a term that describes behaviour which lies outside the social *norms* subscribed to by the majority of a social group and that is likely to attract social disapproval and even punishment.

■ Illegal behaviour, i.e. crime, is deviant, but deviant behaviour is not necessarily illegal. What constitutes deviance will differ, depending on historical period, culture and social group.

■ *e.g.* The law regards the smoking of cannabis as both illegal and deviant, although surveys indicate that young people may regard such behaviour as an acceptable part of their social scene.

deviancy amplification: the process by which the mass media amplify or exaggerate a particular 'problem' or the behaviour of a particular group.

■ In doing so the media create a social reaction which heightens police activity, court sentencing and public awareness in a vicious spiral which bears little relation to the original problem or behaviour. The official reaction, i.e. new laws, more policing and stiffer sentencing, is likely to generate further deviance which provokes a more severe official response and so on.

■ *e.g.* Stan Cohen's ***Folk Devils and Moral Panics***, on the reporting of mods and rockers in the 1960s, is a classic study of deviancy amplification.

deviant career: a concept associated with *labelling theory* in which the behaviour of an individual who has internalised a *master status* of 'criminal' or 'deviant' comes to reflect the deviant label.

■ Part of the problem for deviant individuals is the reaction of society, which may only interpret their behaviour in the light of the label.

■ *e.g.* Those with a criminal record may be denied the opportunity of pursuing a 'normal' career. They may seek solace in the company of those similarly labelled and form a deviant *subculture*.

■ *TIP* Note that this is an example of the *self-fulfilling prophecy* in action — don't just apply that concept to an educational setting.

deviant voter: a working-class or middle-class voter who votes for a political party which does not represent their class interests.

■ Both the Labour Party and the Conservative Party could not win power without a significant number of middle-class and working-class deviant votes respectively.

diary: a type of *personal document* which can be used as a source of *secondary data* or *primary data* for sociological research purposes.

■ Sociologists can use diaries as a means of gaining a historical perspective on a particular social event or problem. In this sense, diaries can be a useful source of secondary data, although such documents always carry the risk of *bias*. Some sociologists ask their research sample to keep diaries documenting their attitudes and feelings.

■ *e.g.* Ann Oakley asked housewives to keep diaries documenting their feelings about housework.

■ *TIP* There are variations upon this theme. See *time-budget studies.*

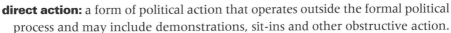

direct action: a form of political action that operates outside the formal political process and may include demonstrations, sit-ins and other obstructive action.

■ In recent years illegal direct action has become more common. Society has seen symbolic attacks on targets such as politicians (throwing paint or eggs at them), damage to nuclear weapons installations or military hardware and the destroying of genetically modified crops. Some animal rights groups have even physically attacked scientists with letter and car bombs.

■ *e.g.* Militant disabled groups have chained themselves to the gates of Downing Street and the Reclaim the Streets movement has severely disrupted traffic in the centre of London.

disability: an impairment in a person's capacity to participate fully in society caused by physical, mental or sensory factors that either limit a person's opportunities to take part in normal activities or lead to barriers to a normal life being imposed upon them by others.

■ In recent years sociologists have taken an interest in how disabled people construct their identities and how society's attitude to disability results in prejudice and discrimination.

■ *e.g.* A social model of disability notes that the disabled are more handicapped by a lack of appropriate social facilities and by negative attitudes than they are by their disability.

disableism: the combination of social forces, cultural values and personal prejudices that marginalise disabled people and portray them in a negative and deviant light.

■ The result of such *stereotyping* is that disabled people come to be seen by the non-disabled purely in terms of their impairment, and social segregation. There have been recent signs that some sections of the disabled are politically mobilising against disableism, which Davies describes as 'the last civil rights battle'.

■ *e.g.* Disableism includes failing to build physical environments in which the disabled can move about freely, institutional discrimination, being stereotyped by both the media and the general public as being ugly, asexual, intellectually impaired, unable to speak for themselves etc. It embodies the widely accepted view that disability equals dependency.

discourse: a set of powerful scientific and specialist *concepts* and beliefs that have become the dominant means of approaching and managing key social and medical problems.

■ Foucault notes how attitudes to both madness and sexual behaviour have been dominated by an interplay of discourse originating in medical science and religion.

discrimination: the putting into practice of prejudicial and stereotypical attitudes which stress the inferiority and/or difference of particular groups via individual or institutional action. (See *racial discrimination*.)

■ *e.g.* Institutional practices may be discriminating in their exclusion of women and/or ethnic minorities from senior occupational positions.

d

disenchantment: see *desacrilisation.*

disengagement (1): the process by which the elderly withdraw from society.

■ *e.g.* Retirement.

disengagement (2): an aspect of *secularisation* which suggests that the church was once heavily involved in politics, education and welfare but has now declined in terms of its power, control and influence.

dispersed extended family: a network of *nuclear families* who are geographically distant from each other but retain frequent contact through the use of the telephone, e-mail, letters and visits.

■ The existence of such families suggests that functionalist ideas about the *relative isolation of the family* may be exaggerated.

division of labour: the way that work is organised into a complex structure of interdependent specialised tasks.

■ Durkheim argues that the division of labour in industrial societies contributes to *social order* because its complexity means that people's actions are both complementary and interdependent. In other words, our dependence on each other to provide specialised skills produces an integrated society.

divorce: the legal termination of a marriage.

■ Most divorce is obtained after an agreed 2-year separation period and is granted on the grounds of irretrievable breakdown of marriage, although a 'quickie' divorce can be obtained after 1 year of marriage if adultery, desertion, physical and mental cruelty etc. can be proved in court. Britain has one of the highest divorce rates in the European Union and this has resulted in some commentators suggesting it is a symptom of a decline in family values.

■ *TIP* Know how divorce fits into the very popular exam topic of the so-called decline in family life.

divorce rate: the number of people getting divorced per 1,000 of the married population.

document: a source of *secondary data* including *personal documents* such as letters, *diaries,* novels and autobiographies and public documents produced by central and local government agencies and other organisations and *mass media reports.*

■ Documents have to be approached by sociologists with caution. Questions of *reliability* and *validity* arise as to their authenticity, credibility, *representativeness* and *objectivity.*

■ *TIP* Note that research which uses documents today will probably use them alongside other methods as part of a *triangulation* approach.

domestic division of labour: the organisation of domestic roles within marriage/*cohabitation.*

■ It was suggested in the 1970s that domestic roles were becoming more *egalitarian* in that men were making a greater contribution to housework and childcare, although empirical studies indicate that equality in domestic roles is probably exaggerated.

domestic labour: refers to all work concerned with maintaining the household.

■ Domestic labour mainly consists of housework, childcare and emotional labour, which is concerned with meeting the family's emotional needs. It is largely unpaid and performed by women.

domestic labour theory: a *Marxist feminist* theory which states that women's unpaid work in the home has an economic value and consequently plays a crucial role in the maintenance of capitalism.

■ Benston argues that the domestic labour of women maintains the health and efficiency of the labour force and reproduces the future labour force at no extra cost to the capitalist class.

domestic violence: a term usually associated with the physical abuse of women by husbands or partners in the home.

■ It is probably impossible accurately to assess the true amount of domestic violence, although sociologists estimate that one in four married women are likely to experience it. Feminists suggest that domestic violence reflects gendered power differences between men and women in that it is still acceptable in *patriarchal* societies for men to exercise control and power over women by using violence.

dominant class: a Marxist term that normally refers to the *capitalist class* although it is sometimes used to refer to the *middle class* in general.

double burden: the double *oppression* faced by black women in terms of being exploited by men and being victims of *racism*.

double standard of sexual morality: the idea that promiscuous behaviour in males should be admired and encouraged whereas the same behaviour in females is condemned and regarded as deviant.

dual burden: refers to dual responsibilities that many women experience within the family in that they generally tend to work either full time or part time yet still take the main responsibility for domestic labour.

dual career family: a family in which both husband and wife have fulfilling professional careers.

■ Such families may be characterised by potential conflict because of the tensions between career and domestic arrangements, especially for women. Many working women find themselves with the *dual burden* of juggling work and domestic responsibilities.

dual labour market: a model of work which suggests that the labour market is split into a *primary sector*, which comprises relatively high-wage jobs with good career prospects, and a *secondary sector*, which contains low-paid, low-skilled and non-unionised jobs.

■ It is argued that males generally monopolise primary sector jobs whilst females and some ethnic minority groups are allocated to the secondary market by employers who subscribe to *patriarchal* and *racist* stereotypes about these social groups.

dual systems theory: a feminist theory which focuses on how *patriarchy* and *capitalism* interact to bring about the oppression of women.

■ This theory notes that capitalism functions to segregate jobs by sex and consequently men benefit from earning more than women. Low wages also encourage dependency on men who benefit in the home from *domestic labour*. However, women's domestic roles serve to weaken their position in the labour market. Capitalism and patriarchy therefore reinforce each other.

dysfunction/dysfunctional: a *functionalist* concept focusing on the negative or harmful effects that a social institution can have on society and individuals.

■ *e.g.* Education can be dysfunctional if it wastes talents by labelling some children as failures.

economic deprivation: see *material deprivation* and *poverty*.

economic determinism: see *economic reductionism*.

economic reductionism: a critique of Marxism which suggests that Marxists over-emphasise the class relationships that arise out of the economic system and consequently ignore or neglect other important sources of inequality such as gender and ethnicity.

■ Also known as economic determinism, this critique is particularly critical of the Marxist trend of reducing all activity in the social institutions that make up the *superstructure* to serving the class relationships that underpin the *infrastructure*. It is suggested that such institutions also operate to maintain gender and racial inequalities.

ecumenical movement: a movement attempting to achieve greater unity between various Christian denominations.

■ Some sociologists who support the *secularisation* thesis, e.g. Wilson, see it as a symptom of weakness in religion, because it is a response to declining attendance and membership.

Educational Priority Area (EPA): an inner-city area characterised by economic and social deprivation that was selected in the 1960s for extra educational resourcing. There were six EPAs.

■ The rationale for such positive discrimination was the *cultural deprivation* idea of *compensatory education* — that education could compensate for the disadvantages arising out of poverty.

■ *TIP* Note the similarity between EPAs and the education action zones created by Labour in 2000.

Education Reform Act (1988): the most important piece of educational policy since 1944, which resulted in more centralised state regulation of education, greater diversity of educational institutions and an attempt to create greater choice for parents.

■ The *national curriculum*, testing at 7, 11 and 14, *city technology colleges, league tables, grant-maintained schools* and *open enrolment* were all products of this act.

egalitarianism: a value system dominated by the goal of equality which, depending on sociological perspective, may relate to opportunity, outcome or reward.

- Some sociologists, especially Marxists and feminists, are committed to bringing about an egalitarian society.
- *TIP* Wilmott and Young suggested that modern marriage was egalitarian but empirical studies do not support this view.

egoistic suicide: a type of suicide identified by Durkheim, allegedly caused by excessive *individualism*.

- Durkheim argued that such suicide was apparent in societies that lack *social integration*, i.e. the bond between the individual and society is slack.
- *e.g.* Durkheim saw the higher suicide rate of Protestant societies as a result of that church encouraging 'free enquiry' and being less community-orientated than the Catholic Church.
- *TIP* Suicide is regarded as a type of *deviance* in Western societies.

elaborated code: a type of *language code* identified by Basil Bernstein and allegedly partially responsible for the superior achievement of middle-class pupils in the school environment, because it is used by teachers to communicate instruction and knowledge.

- *Cultural deprivation theory* has used Bernstein's work to suggest that the working class suffer from *linguistic deprivation*.
- *e.g.* Working-class children's alleged lack of access to the elaborated code, which is rich in adverbs/adjectives and deals comfortably with concepts, is seen to put them at a serious educational disadvantage.
- *TIP* This concept should be discussed alongside the *restricted code*.

electoral register: a list of those eligible to vote (i.e. aged over 18) kept by local authorities and often used as a *sampling frame* by sociologists.

- *TIP* Its *reliability* as a sampling frame is undermined by the absence of specific groups, i.e. those aged under 18, the homeless, those who do not register etc.

eleven-plus/11+ examination: a type of *intelligence* test taken at 11 years of age to determine whether a child should attend a *grammar school*, a technical school or a *secondary modern school*.

- Such tests were thought to discriminate in favour of middle-class children who had the *cultural capital* to cope successfully with the sorts of knowledge and skills demanded of them. These tests were largely abandoned in the 1960s as local education authorities switched from the *tripartite system* to *comprehensive schools*, although they are still used in some areas to ascertain the suitability of grammar school candidates.

elite: often referred to by elite theorists as the best and most talented in a society but by *critical sociologists* as a small minority group that dominates a society by virtue of its wealth.

- Classical elite theory tends to suggest that elites are natural leaders who are born to rule because of superior intelligence, breeding etc. Marxists and others such as C. Wright Mills are sceptical about such characteristics (see *power elite*).
- *e.g.* Marxists argue that there exists a capitalist ruling class made up of economic elites (i.e. capitalist businessmen) and political elites (i.e. politicians)

who are united by common ties (i.e. social class background, wealth, public schools and Oxbridge, clubs etc.) and common goals (i.e. reproducing and maintaining inequality).

■ *TIP* John Scott's work on 'the *establishment*' is an excellent source on elites in the UK.

elite theory: mainly associated with the work of Pareto and Mosca, this theory observes that the few (i.e. elites) have always dominated the many.

■ Elite theorists believe democracy is dangerous because the masses have not got the skills required to rule effectively.

■ *e.g.* Pareto argued that power is best managed by elites, whether they be 'foxes' (i.e. those who rule by cunning) or 'lions' (i.e. those who rule by military strength).

■ *TIP* Both *pluralism* and *Marxism* should be contrasted with this theory as evaluation.

embourgeoisement: a theory, popularised by Zweig in the 1960s, which claimed that increased affluence had led to many working-class manual workers adopting the lifestyle and culture of the middle class, so undermining traditional working-class identity.

■ The theory was empirically tested by Goldthorpe and Lockwood's *affluent worker study* which concluded that there was some *convergence* in terms of *consumption* patterns but that the values of the working class and middle class remained very different. However, embourgeoisement as a concept continued to prosper in the 1980s and can be seen particularly in the work of Ivor Crewe on voting behaviour.

■ *TIP* See Fiona Divine's **The Affluent Worker Revisited** (1992) for an update on this debate.

emigration: the movement of people out of a country or region on a permanent basis.

■ Between 1870 and 1930 there were more people leaving the UK than entering it. Since 1962 more people have left the UK than entered it. Most have emigrated to Australia and New Zealand, the USA and Canada, although the most popular destination has been Europe.

emotion work: an aspect of women's domestic work which involves recognising the emotional needs of other family members and responding to them.

■ Duncombe and Marsden found that many women held marriages and family together by doing the emotion work.

■ *e.g.* They found that men were able to express emotional satisfaction through their work but were unable or unwilling to discuss feelings and emotions with their wives. Women therefore experienced dissatisfaction with men's lack of emotional input into the relationship. However, many were willing to maintain the illusion of a happy family for the sake of the children.

■ *TIP* The concept of emotion work is a useful counter-argument to use in order to challenge the view that conjugal roles are egalitarian.

empathetic understanding: see *verstehen*.

empathy: the ability to feel what others are experiencing.

■ In sociology it is generally associated with *interpretivist* approaches that aim to uncover how people interpret social situations. Interpretivists champion the Weberian idea of *verstehen* or empathetic understanding.

■ *e.g.* The preferred research methods of interpretivists, such as observation and unstructured interviewing, aim to get inside the heads of those being researched in order to see the world through their eyes.

empirical: scientific/sociological investigation based on evidence collected in the natural or social world.

■ Sociology is often unfairly criticised for focusing on abstract *theory* or conjecture, but a good deal of sociology is research-based and concerned with empirical evidence, i.e. things that can be observed, measured and tested.

employment relations: a concept used by the *NS-SEC* method of classifying occupations into social classes that takes into consideration whether people are employers, self-employed, employed, temporary or casual workers, whether they exercise authority over others etc.

empty-nest family: a family in which the children have grown up and left home.

empty-shell marriage: a form of marital breakdown in which the couple retain the legal ties but lack the characteristics such as love and intimacy that are normally associated with a happy marriage.

■ The couple may be staying together for the sake of the children or because their religion forbids or disapproves of divorce. The extent of this type of marital breakdown is extremely difficult to estimate.

endogamy: a form of social control that ensures the practice of marriage within the social group to which people belong.

■ It is normally associated with societies in which social groups (e.g. tribes, religions, ethnic groups etc.) compete against each other for scarce resources.

EPA: see *Educational Priority Area*.

equality: the state of being equal, especially relative to other individuals or social groups.

■ *Critical sociologists* are generally concerned with uncovering social inequalities based on social class, gender, race and ethnicity, disability, age and sexuality, and working towards societies in which all social groups share the same opportunities and outcomes.

equality of opportunity: the view that all members of society should have the same opportunities to succeed.

■ The principle underpins *social democratic* thinking on education, health, the welfare state and workplace practices. It is generally regarded as the foundation stone of *meritocratic* societies, in that people have an equal chance to become unequal.

■ *TIP* A good deal of educational policy (e.g. the *tripartite system, comprehensive schools, compensatory education* and female-friendly initiatives) was based on this principle.

equality of outcome: the principle underpinning the notion of *egalitarianism* which states that all should share equally in the rewards of society.

■ The most egalitarian type of society is communist. Some people believe that *positive discrimination* is required to ensure equality of outcome because some groups (e.g. women and ethnic minorities) are handicapped by the way society is organised.

Essex man: see *new working class*.

Essex mobility study: a project led by G. Marshall and based on a sample of 1,770 adults in 1988 that collected data about male and female *social mobility* rates.

■ It concluded that the *relative rate of mobility* had worsened since the *Oxford mobility study*.

■ *e.g.* The researchers found that someone starting in the *service class* had a seven-times greater chance than a working-class person of ending up in the service class. Moreover, the destinations of women were found to be less advantageous compared with men.

■ *TIP* Note that Saunders accuses the researchers of ideological *bias*.

establishment: a term used to describe those who dominate the top positions in society in business, politics, the civil service, the military, judiciary etc.

■ Some sociologists refer to those groups as *elites*, whilst Marxists suggest they are aggregated into a *ruling class*.

■ *e.g.* J. Scott notes the existence of a *power elite* or establishment in the UK dominated by a capitalist class which occupies key positions in the state and which is able to exert a strong influence on government economic policy.

ethical constraints: the view, accepted by the majority of sociologists, that social research should be regulated by ethical rules.

■ Some generally agreed ethical guidelines include the idea that people should not be physically, socially or psychologically harmed or disadvantaged by research.

■ *e.g.* It is generally agreed that research should not involve the invasion of privacy and should only take place with the consent of those taking part. Anonymity and confidentiality should be guaranteed if required. Some research methods, notably observation, are criticised for neglecting some of these guidelines.

■ *TIP* Think about how the existence of such guidelines undermines the idea of *value freedom* in sociology.

ethical deprivation: a concept used by Glock and Stark to explain why some members of society join religious *sects*.

■ Ethical deprivation is the result of people perceiving the world to be in moral decline. They may retreat into *introversionist* sects.

■ *e.g.* Jim Jones' People's Temple retreated into the jungle of Guyana where approximately 800 of its members committed mass suicide.

ethnic identity: the sense of *identity* and interest that derives from sharing common factors such as descent, language, history, heritage, religion, traditions, as well as the shared experience of coming into daily contact with the majority culture and its institutions.

■ *e.g.* Sociologists note that *institutional racism* and the everyday *prejudice* and discrimination embodied in actions such as racist name-calling have resulted in young members of some ethnic minority groups rejecting British identity. They have turned instead to alternative identities based on religion (e.g. Islam), fashion or music such as gangsta rap and hip hop etc. as a form of symbolic protest against racism. Other studies, e.g. Johal, note that young Asians are combining elements of traditional Asian and British identities to form hybrid cultures.

ethnicity: a type of cultural distinctiveness associated with a particular ethnic group.

■ Members of ethnic populations identify with each other because they share common factors such as descent, language, history, heritage, traditions etc.

■ *e.g.* *Socialisation* into ethnic identity clearly marks out the position of one ethnic group in relation to others, and gives members a strong sense of cultural identity. Some sociologists such as Johal have noted that ethnicity may be diluted by the emergence of *hybrid cultures* in *multicultural* societies.

■ *TIP* Think about how agencies of socialisation such as the family and religion may socialise people into their ethnic identity.

ethnic minority: in the UK, a term generally referring to people who originated in the former British colonies of the Indian subcontinent and the Caribbean.

■ Such a definition focuses on colour and generally for many people it means 'not white'. This definition ignores the large communities of white ethnic minorities found in the UK, e.g. Jewish, Irish, Cypriot, Italian etc.

■ *TIP* Studies of ethnic minority inequalities in the sociology of *stratification* mainly focus on African-Caribbean and Asian people, but these studies fail to acknowledge that these broad groups are composed of a range of different ethnic minority groups whose experiences vary.

ethnocentric: the judgement that one social group has a superior culture or way of doing things compared with another.

■ Ethnocentrism involves two processes: first, judging particular cultures as deficient and consequently concluding that they have no value; and second, insisting that the culture to which those making the judgement belong (usually middle-class, white and Western) is morally and socially superior, usually while conveniently ignoring the social problems associated with that culture.

■ *TIP* Note that *cultural deprivation theory* in the fields of health and education and *modernisation theory* can be accused of being ethnocentric.

ethnography: sociological research that is conducted in the natural environment of the research subjects and describes their way of life.

■ The most common ethnographic methods are *participant observation*, although in-depth *case studies*, *life histories*, *time-budget* and *community studies* are all variations upon this theme. All are aimed at exploring how research subjects construct and interpret their social reality, and consequently are preferred by *interpretivist* sociologists.

ethnomethodology: a specialised *interpretivist* approach that aims to analyse how people construct and make sense of routine social activity by uncovering the rules that govern all social interactions and situations.

■ This approach generally believes that the order that characterises our routine everyday experience is achieved by our sharing of complex, unwritten, taken-for-granted rules.

■ *e.g.* Garfinkel's ethnomethodological experiments aimed to uncover the taken-for-granted rules of family life by breaking them. This approach believes that all routine practices are governed by rules but we only become aware of them when they break down.

exogamy: a system of marriage in which people can only marry people from outside their social or kinship group.

■ *TIP* Always contrast this concept with *endogamy*.

experiment: the manipulation of variables in a controlled environment in order to establish a causal relationship.

■ In the *natural sciences*, the laboratory method is the classic research method. It normally involves the setting up of an experimental group which is subjected to various influences and compared with a control group. The differences between the two groups provide evidence for causal relationships between *independent variables* (causes) and *dependent variables* (effects). However, such experiments are rarely used in sociological research for ethical reasons and because it is regarded as impossible to find human control and experimental groups that are exactly alike.

■ *e.g.* We could never be sure that differences in behaviour were not due to differences in interpretation or due to the *Hawthorne effect*.

experimental effect: see *Hawthorne effect*.

exploitation: the appropriation of the skills and labour of less powerful groups without rewarding them.

■ Marxists use the term to refer to the appropriation of the *surplus value* of the labour of the working class by the capitalist class. This is the basis of the great inequalities in income and wealth and therefore underpins class inequality. Feminists see male appropriation of women's skills and labour as a major aspect of *patriarchy*.

expressive leader: a term used by Parsons in his theory of the family and gender roles to describe the feminine role of nurturer and emotional caretaker within the *nuclear family* unit.

■ Parsons argues that for the family to function effectively there must be a *sexual division of labour* in which males and females occupy specific and distinct roles that complement each other and make an equally important input into family stability. Parsons subscribed to the *biological determinist* view regarding the role of females.

■ *e.g.* He believed that females were genetically predisposed to be responsible for the *primary socialisation* of the young and relieving the stress of the male breadwinner with love, housekeeping skills and sexual pleasure. Feminists are extremely critical of this idea. They argue that such roles are socially constructed rather than biologically inherited through the process of *gender role socialisation*.

■ *TIP* Any discussion of expressive leaders should also make reference to *instrumental leaders*.

extended family: a family that contains relatives beyond the core of the *nuclear family* unit living in the same house, street or area.

■ A family which contains at least three generations (e.g. grandparents, parents and children) under the same roof or in the immediate neighbourhood is known as a vertical extended family. Families which contain aunts, uncles and cousins living under the same roof are horizontal extended families. Some sociologists have suggested that some nuclear families can be defined as *modified extended* or *dispersed extended* or *attenuated extended*, based on their contact with extended kin.

■ *e.g.* Janet Foster documents examples of the classic vertical extended family in the East End of London in the 1980s, whilst Sikhs tend to live in horizontal extended families.

extrinsic satisfaction: the view that people mainly work for financial reward rather than for *work satisfaction*.

■ It is seen to be a characteristic of *instrumentalist* workers.

false consciousness: a Marxist term suggesting that workers do not see the true nature of their exploitation or the fact that they have common interests because of the influence of *ideology*.

■ Marxists see social agencies such as education, mass media and religion as promoting ruling-class ideology and thus disguising the true level of class inequality and *exploitation* in capitalist societies.

false need: the outcome of sustained advertising which convinces people that a consumer item is vital to their social well-being, although in reality the item is merely a symbol of *conspicuous consumption*.

■ Illich is particularly concerned about the commercial promotion by multinational companies of false needs in the developing world, as he believes that they contribute to poor levels of health.

■ *e.g.* Advertising of potential health-damaging consumer items such as cigarettes, soft drinks such as Coca-Cola, baby milk powder etc. persuade people in the developing world that these items are essential elements of a Western lifestyle which they should adopt if they wish to be modern.

falsification: the seeking of evidence in order to show a *hypothesis* to be false rather than gathering evidence in support of it.

■ Karl Popper argued that no amount of evidence gathered can prove a hypothesis or *conjecture* true. There is always the possibility that a piece of evidence will eventually appear that refutes the hypothesis. Popper therefore suggested that scientific research should systematically attempt to falsify theory.

■ *TIP* Popper suggested that sociology was overly theoretical and consequently not enough *empirical* research or falsification went on for it to qualify as scientific.

familistic ideology: a set of ideas about what constitutes 'good' family life that is responsible for a nuclear family blueprint publicised by the media and politicians, which we are all encouraged to live up to.

■ This ideology sees as ideal the 'conventional' nuclear family of husband, wife and a small number of unmarried dependent children.

■ *e.g.* Supporters of this ideology stress the importance of marriage as the moral foundation stone underpinning family life. The traditional domestic division of labour in which the mother stays at home looking after the children is also preferred and consequently working mothers are seen as a cause of social problems. Departures from this nuclear stereotype — in particular, *one-parent families, cohabitation, divorce* and single-sex couples — often give rise to concerns about declining morality and the suggestion from *New Right* commentators that 'proper' family life is in decline.

family: an intimate domestic group composed of people related to each other by blood, sexual relations and legal ties.

■ The Sociology of the Family has recently been dominated by a debate between traditionalists and *postmodernists*. The former see the family as best defined in terms of the nuclear unit whilst the latter suggest that no one type of family should be the dominant type — rather diversity and variation are the norm in both family structure and internal relationships.

■ *TIP* Whether sociologists believe that the family is in decline depends on whether they adopt the traditionalist or postmodern definition of family.

family diversity: the fact that modern UK society is now characterised by a range of family types with diverse internal arrangements rather than the *nuclear family* model.

■ Family life in the UK is now dominated by organisational diversity, i.e. other family types have evolved alongside or out of the nuclear family. Cultural diversity means that there are differences in family lifestyle because of ethnic origin and differences in religious beliefs. Family life is also diverse in relation to internal domestic arrangements, i.e. how couples interact with each other and their children, and their relationships with extended kinship networks.

■ *e.g.* The growth of *one-parent families, reconstituted families, dual-career families* and single-sex couples are all examples of family diversity in the modern UK.

■ *TIP* Family diversity is a useful means of challenging the *New Right* idea that family life is in decline because it suggests that family life is evolving rather than deteriorating.

fatalistic suicide: a type of suicide identified by Durkheim, allegedly caused by excessive regulation of the individual.

■ Such suicide is the result of too many social controls and oppressive discipline.

■ *e.g.* Prison suicides may be caused by individuals failing to cope with excessive regulation and control.

female underachievement: the trend, especially in the period prior to the 1990s, for females to perform less well in the hard sciences and mathematics, to be over-represented in stereotypically feminine subjects and to be generally under-represented in higher education.

■ There is evidence that since the 1990s females have been performing considerably better than males at all levels of education, although there are still concerns about gendered subject choice, especially in higher education.

■ *TIP* Know why female achievement has improved and why allegedly there is now *male underachievement*.

femininity: characteristics and behaviour patterns that have been traditionally defined as socially appropriate for females.

■ The nature of femininity has long been debated, as has *masculinity,* as part of the *nature versus nurture debate,* i.e. between those who see femininity as determined by biology and feminist sociologists who see it as socially constructed via *gender role socialisation.* Today femininity is widely accepted as being the product of both biological and cultural influences.

■ *TIP* Note the emergence of alternative forms of femininity, e.g. career women and lesbianism.

feminisation of labour: the process whereby certain jobs and employment sectors, especially those previously monopolised by men, have become dominated by female workers.

■ There are two sociological interpretations of this process. First, the *colonisation* of particular occupational sectors, e.g. teaching, nursing and clerical work, is seen to lower the status and consequently the wage levels of those sectors. Second, feminist observers suggest such feminisation has resulted in economic independence for many women and a consequent increase in social and cultural power, which has implications for the organisation of the domestic division of labour, marriage rates, divorce etc.

■ *TIP* Think about how working women may demand more from marriage compared with housewives.

feminisation of poverty: the fact that women are more likely than men to experience poverty.

■ This is due to the increasing number of *one-parent families* (mainly headed by women) and the fact that childcare commitments mean that women are more likely to be in part-time and/or lower-paid jobs compared with men. Additionally, women are more likely to outlive men into old age, and pensioners are one of the groups most likely to fall into poverty.

feminism: a set of sociological theories that aim to describe and explain the position of women in society.

■ Although feminist theories differ in explanation, they share common ground in that they see modern societies as *patriarchal.*

■ *e.g.* They see gender roles as largely socially constructed via the *socialisation* process and resulting in the domination of males and the subordination of females.

■ *TIP* Despite the variation in feminist thought, note that feminist theories share similar weaknesses, especially the tendency to be *over-deterministic* in their view of how women respond to patriarchy.

fertility rate: the number of actual child births in a population per thousand women of child-bearing age.

■ The evidence suggests that fertility rates have declined in the West as standards of living have improved and the costs of children have risen. The failure of fertility rates to fall in the *less developed world* as mortality rates have fallen is probably responsible for rising population in those parts of the world.

feudalism: a type of *stratification* system based on ownership of land characteristic of medieval Europe.

■ This was a hierarchical system with the monarch and his or her nobles
controlling ownership of agricultural land whilst at the bottom of society the
mass of peasants had few rights. Feudal societies were *closed societies* in that
there was little opportunity for *social mobility*. European feudal societies
eventually gave way to industrial societies based on relationships between
those who owned the means of industrial production and workers, i.e.
capitalism.

field experiment: an experiment carried out in a natural setting because the
subject matter is unsuitable for study under laboratory conditions.

■ Two examples of field experiments are the *Hawthorne* experiment carried out
by Elton Mayo in the 1920s and Rosenthal and Jacobsen's 1960s experiment
into the *self-fulfilling prophecy*.

first world: see *developed world*.

flexible specialisation theory: see *post-Fordism*.

folk devils: a concept developed by Stan Cohen that describes those groups
identified and stereotyped by the mass media through the sensationalist
reporting associated with *moral panics* as posing a threat to society.

■ Cohen suggests that the mass media particularly demonised youth cultures
such as mods, rockers, skinheads and punks. Some groups may be subjected
to heavier social controls by the government and agencies of law and order as
a result of such media attention.

■ *e.g.* The recent demonisation of the rap star Eminem.

Fordism: a system of mass industrial production based on assembly lines situated
in large factories.

■ Fordism essentially took control away from workers and put it in the hands of
management.

■ *e.g.* Management defined how something would be manufactured, decided
the speed of its manufacture and imposed targets on workers. Fordism also led
to complex skills being broken down and simplified and consequently a decline
in the skill-level, status and pay of previously skilled craftsmen.

■ *TIP* Marxists argue that such production and management practices have
increased *deskilling* and *alienation*.

formal economy: that part of the economy made up of paid jobs in which people
declare and pay tax and make national insurance contributions as opposed to
the black or *informal economy*.

formal interview: see *structured interview*.

foundation school: see *grant-maintained school*.

Frankfurt School: a group of German Marxists, e.g. Theodor Adorno, Herbert
Marcuse etc., who argued that the capitalist ruling class use the mass media
and *popular culture* in an ideological way to shape society's thinking, thus
ensuring passive conformity and *false consciousness*.

- Marcuse argued that *popular* or *mass culture* such as Hollywood films, pop music and television serve to convince the masses that consumption of capitalist products is all-important and to devalue critical and creative thinking.
- *e.g.* Popular culture supposedly contains within it ideological messages that the population internalises as normal and natural, thus ensuring ruling-class cultural domination or *hegemony*.

free will: the theory, associated with *interpretivists*, that people have consciousness and are therefore responsible for their own social reality because they are able to exercise choice over their actions.

- This is generally an *anti-positivist* stance, since it implicitly rejects the notion that social behaviour is determined by external influences.

function: the usefulness or benefit derived from an agency or activity for the general maintenance of society.

- Generally, institutions such as the family and education are seen by *functionalists* as functioning for the good of society in that they positively contribute to *value consensus* and *social integration*, thus ensuring *social order*.
- *TIP* This concept should be contrasted with *dysfunction*.

functionalism: a sociological perspective that sees modern Western societies as characterised by *social order* and *consensus*.

- Functionalists argue that the function of institutions such as the family, education, religion etc. is to reproduce culture by socialising individuals into the key values and roles required for social stability. Functionalism is a *structuralist* theory, because it believes that the way society is organised is responsible for the maintenance of social order. It is also *positivist*, because it believes that human behaviour is determined by factors external to the individual (e.g. *value consensus*).
- *TIP* Be aware of the similarities and differences of this theory compared with Marxism.

functional prerequisites: the basic needs or requirements that must be met according to *functionalists* if societies are to survive.

- These include production of food and shelter, a system of *socialisation* and communication, a degree of *social integration*, control of potentially disruptive behaviour, and *social order*.

fundamentalism: the belief, usually religious in character, in the need to subscribe or return to traditional values and practices.

- It is particularly associated with Islam, although in the USA it is associated with Protestant Christianity (e.g. the 'bible belt'). It usually involves the literal interpretation of a holy text (e.g. the Bible or Koran).
- *e.g.* In Islamic countries, fundamentalist belief may influence all aspects of society, e.g. politics, art, relations between men and women etc.
- *TIP* It is easy to devalue or dismiss fundamentalism as 'extreme' or 'fanatical' from a Western perspective. A good sociologist should not judge but should attempt to analyse objectively the context in which it appears.

gate-keepers (1): those who control entry to certain occupational sectors.

■ Feminists believe that one reason why women are under-represented in professional and managerial positions is because male gate-keepers deny entry to them and so sustain the *glass ceiling*.

gate-keepers (2): used in the sociology of the mass media to describe those, usually editors, who define what counts as news.

■ Marxists argue that capitalist owners of the media and their agents, i.e. editors and journalists, set the agenda for public debate and knowledge by including some types of stories as news and excluding others. This gate-keeping allegedly functions to benefit capitalism ideologically by shaping what the general public thinks about critical issues.

■ *e.g.* Those issues and values defined by the gate-keepers as outside the mainstream may be excluded or derided as 'extreme'.

■ *TIP* Compare this view with the pluralist position that gate-keeping is merely a consequence of making a professional decision as to whether a story is newsworthy or not.

Gemeinschaft: a concept developed by Tönnies to describe societies that are characterised by a strong sense of *community* and *social order*, e.g. rural societies.

■ Such societies tend to be small-scale. Roles are generally ascribed, i.e. people are valued for what they are rather than for what they do. There is a limited division of labour, as people tend to inherit occupational roles. The culture of such societies tends to be characterised by traditional values and there are clear-cut rules about behaviour that are strongly enforced by institutions like the family and the church.

■ *TIP* Discussion of Gemeinschaft should also make reference to *Gesellschaft*.

gender: the social and psychological characteristics associated with *femininity* and *masculinity*, which are thought to be the product of the cultural expectations of particular societies, learnt through the process of *gender role socialisation*.

■ Sociologists distinguish between 'sex', meaning the biological or physiological differences between males and females, i.e. genitalia, and 'gender', meaning the behavioural differences.

g

■ *e.g.* In Western society, men are supposed to be sexually promiscuous whilst women are supposed to be sexually passive.

■ *TIP* Gender is seen as one of the key forms of *stratification* in modern societies, as reflected in differentiation between the sexes in occupational mobility, pay, family roles etc.

gender identity: the sense of *self* that is associated with cultural expectations about *masculinity* and *femininity* into which we are socialised through contact with agencies such as the family, media etc.

■ There is some evidence that traditional gender identities may be undergoing change. Traditional notions of masculinity that revolve around, for example, being the breadwinner may be challenged by the *feminisation of labour*, the decline in traditional male industries and the consequent *crisis of masculinity*.

■ *e.g.* New forms of femininity may be arising as females acquire economic independence from men and take advantage of a greater range of choices in education, employment, consumption etc.

genderquake: a phrase invented by Helen Wilkinson to describe what she sees as a fundamental shift in values among the female under-35 age-group relating to women's role in society, which has supposedly resulted in a shift of power from men to women.

■ This alleged change is rooted in the feminisation of the workplace, which has had consequences for women's attitudes towards the family.

■ *e.g.* Wilkinson argues that work and career are increasingly more important than marriage and children to a woman's identity and self-esteem. Traditional notions of femininity therefore are being abandoned as young women adopt risk-taking behaviour traditionally associated with males.

gender role socialisation: the social process by which children learn their *gender* roles.

■ From an early age, people are trained to conform to social expectations with regard to gender behaviour. Much of this training goes on in the family. Parents use gender-orientated terms of endearment when talking to children. They dress boys and girls differently and give them sex-typed toys.

■ *e.g.* Oakley (1981) notes that parents encourage or discourage behaviour on the basis of appropriateness for the sex and they channel children's interests into toys and activities seen as normal for that sex. These types of gender reinforcement are extremely powerful. Evidence suggests that by the age of five, most children have acquired a clear gender identity.

■ *TIP* Secondary agents of socialisation such as education and the mass media also make a significant contribution to gender role socialisation.

gender stereotyping: the process by which the behaviour and attitudes of males and females are defined in exaggerated and over-simplified ways so that they are generalised to all males and females.

gender stratification: the division of society into a hierarchy based on differential opportunities and rewards according to gender, which benefits males at the expense of females.

■ Feminist sociologists refer to such societies as *patriarchies*. There is some debate as to the importance of gender as a source of stratification. Some sociologists see *social class* and *ethnicity* as more or equally important.

■ *TIP* Gender interacts with social class and ethnicity to produce the stratification system that characterises the modern UK.

generalisation: the application of findings from a representative *sample* to the wider social group to which the sample belongs.

■ It is possible to suggest that if the sample population behave in a particular way, the larger group from which the sample was drawn will behave similarly.

generalised other: expectations relating to *norms* and *values* that define and govern our behaviour and social *identity* as members of a particular social group.

■ Society expects people to behave in particular ways according to their social and occupational roles, e.g. in the UK we expect mothers to love their children, and husbands and wives to be faithful to each other etc. Therefore when we take on these roles, we usually conform to these expectations.

General National Vocational Qualification: see *GNVQ*.

generation: the division of society's members into age-groups that share a common experience of growing up at the same point in history.

■ The experience of being a member of a particular age-group differs from generation to generation.

gentrification: the trend among young, affluent, middle-class people to buy and renovate terraced properties in economically deprived inner-city areas, especially in London.

geographical mobility: the movement of people to areas in which there are jobs or where particular skills are in demand.

■ The functionalist theory of the family sees geographical mobility as a crucial influence on the *nuclear family* breaking free of *extended family* networks in the period immediately following the Industrial Revolution. In criticism, the historian Peter Laslett speculates that nuclear families were geographically mobile in the preindustrial period and this aided the speed of industrialisation in the UK.

Gesellschaft: a concept developed by Tönnies to describe societies that are characterised by a weak sense of *community* and *social order*, e.g. urban societies.

■ Such societies tend to be large-scale and characterised by constant change caused by greater social and *geographical mobility*. There is a specialised *division of labour* and consequently relationships between people are primarily economic. Such societies are likely to be culturally diverse. However, rules about behaviour are not so clear-cut and conflict and crime may be the norm rather than consensus and social order.

■ *TIP* Discussion of Gesellschaft should include reference to *Gemeinschaft*.

Glasgow University Media Group: a team of researchers who have investigated the content of both television and print journalism from a Marxist perspective and concluded that the way news is gathered and reported supports the status quo and therefore capitalist interests.

■ *TIP* Recently the GUMG has produced work on media effects and representations of ethnic minority groups.

glass ceiling: a metaphorical term, used mainly by feminists, describing an invisible symbolic barrier that prevents women from breaking through to professional and managerial jobs and achieving the same career goals and pay as similarly qualified men.

glass walls: a metaphorical term that describes the *horizontal segregation* of men and women into different sectors of work.

■ A survey by the Equal Opportunities Commission in 1996 concluded that women in the public sector were mainly employed in health and education, especially nursing and primary school teaching respectively. In the *private sector*, women are over-concentrated in clerical, administrative, retail and personal services such as catering.

■ *TIP* Discussion of inequalities in female employment should also make reference to *vertical segregation* and the *glass ceiling*.

globalisation: the theory that the development of social, cultural and especially economic relationships on a global scale has created a single social order or world system that has profound negative consequences for national identities and individual lifestyles.

■ The boundaries between *nation states* may become less important as *transnational companies* and international financial markets increasingly dominate world trade, and economic recession and unemployment become global trends.

■ *e.g.* Cultural products such as films and music are increasingly produced for the global market and there are fears that these may result in a homogeneous mass entertainment culture that erodes national and ethnic identities.

■ *TIP* *Postmodern* arguments tend to view globalisation as a significant factor in the trend towards *consumption* as a source of *identity*.

GNVQ (General National Vocational Qualification): a vocationally orientated course available to post-16 students in schools and colleges.

■ *New Right* sociologists see such qualifications as part of the *new vocationalism* introduced into schools in the 1980s that reflects the close functional relationship between education and the economy.

goal: an aim, target or result that an individual or collective action strives to attain.

■ Some sociologists believe that societies set goals for their members but their non-attainment leads to deviance.

■ *e.g.* Merton argued that crime and deviance results from the gap between cultural goals and the means available to achieve those goals. He argued that the main social goal of material success was impossible for all to achieve because the institutional means, e.g. education, jobs etc., could not provide everyone with qualifications or well-paid jobs. Merton argued that crime was merely people turning to illegitimate means to pursue the socially acceptable goal of material success.

going native: the possibility that a researcher undertaking *participant observation* (especially in its covert form) will become over-involved with the research subjects and so lose the *objectivity* and detachment that is a crucial aspect of his or her role.

GP fund-holder: a general practitioner who became responsible for his or her own budgets and could purchase services from hospital trusts on behalf of his or her patients, as a consequence of Conservative reform of the NHS in the 1980s.

■ The policy was based on the idea that the principles of the free market, such as competition between health trusts, would promote efficiency and reduce costs. However, evidence suggests that fund-holding leads to a two-tier service.

■ *e.g.* The majority of middle-class patients are registered with doctors in rural or suburban practices where demand on funds is not so great. Heavily subscribed practices in inner-city areas face intensive demands on their funds and are unable to provide the range of services provided by rural practices.

grammar school: a type of state school created by the 1944 Education Act (Butler's Act) for the most academic 20% of children, who were selected by means of the *eleven-plus examination*.

■ However, a disproportionate number of middle-class pupils passed the eleven-plus compared with working-class pupils. Critics of the grammar schools argued that the examination was culturally biased in favour of the middle class and/or middle-class children had material and cultural supports that put them at an advantage compared with working-class children. In 1965 local education authorities were instructed by the Labour government to replace grammar schools and *secondary moderns* with *comprehensive schools*. However, some authorities refused and there are still approximately 130 grammar schools in existence today.

grant-maintained school: a type of school that, under the 1988 Education Reform Act, was allowed to 'opt out' of local authority control after a parental vote and receive finance directly from central government.

■ Such schools were afforded a great deal of day-to-day freedom and consequently some introduced selection by interview. When Labour took power in 1997, grant-maintained schools were renamed 'foundation schools'. They have been returned to local authority funding but still retain special status and consequently have a great deal of autonomy in how they recruit and select pupils.

guided conversation: see *unstructured interview*.

habitus: a concept used by the Marxist sociologist Bourdieu to describe how children of the dominant class learn to appreciate those elements of thought, taste and lifestyle that make up the everyday culture of their class.

■ Middle-class children learn to distinguish between *high culture*, associated with certain types of literature, music, theatre etc., and low or *popular culture*. This is part of the process of transmitting *cultural capital* from one generation to the next. Such cultural capital, alongside economic advantages, gives children of the dominant class crucial advantages over children from the working class in the educational system.

halo effect: the effect of positive labelling by teachers when a pupil can do no wrong in the eyes of a teacher despite engaging in negative activity.

■ This effect is an aspect of the *self-fulfilling prophecy* identified by *symbolic interactionist* sociologists working in the field of education.

hard statistics: those statistics, usually collected by government (i.e. official) agencies, that are regarded by *positivist* sociologists as having been collected in a reliable, objective and scientific way, e.g. registration data relating to births, marriage, divorce and deaths.

■ However, *interpretivist* sociologists argue that hard statistics are subject to some serious problems of both *reliability* and *validity*.

■ *e.g.* Divorce statistics only give us a partial picture of marital breakdown, and suicide statistics may tell us more about coroners' interpretations of certain types of death than about the intentions of the deceased person.

Hawthorne effect: an experimental effect in which the presence and interest of the experimenter is found to be the major cause of the behaviour of the research subject.

■ The effect was discovered by Elton Mayo's research at the Western Electric Company of Chicago in the 1920s. He aimed to examine the possible effect of variables such as light and heat on industrial production at Western Electric's Hawthorne plant.

■ *e.g.* Mayo found that regardless of what changes were made in working conditions, output went up. He concluded that the workers were responding to being involved in the experiment and wished to please the experimenters.

The research therefore was the most important variable.

■ *TIP* The problem can be applied to most forms of sociological research.

head of household: traditionally this was defined as the senior male or breadwinner and consequently, in the *Registrar-General's classification of occupations*, the senior male earner of a family was used as the basis for defining the *social class* of that family.

■ However, the *feminisation of labour* and the decline in traditional male occupations has led to the female wage becoming just as important to family lifestyle as the male wage.

■ *TIP* The concept of *cross-class families* should be used to criticise the use of 'head of household' in defining and measuring social class.

health: the World Health Organisation defines health as a state of complete physical, mental and social well-being and not merely the absence of disease and infirmity.

■ Sociologists see health as a relative concept, because different social groups and societies interpret health and illness in different ways. Definitions of health and illness can also change over time. Health, however, is usually objectively measured across social class, gender, ethnicity and region by reference to *mortality* and *morbidity rates.*

health gap: in 1987 the Health Education Council published ***The Health Divide — Inequalities in Health in the 1980s***, which concluded that while there had been a general improvement in the nation's health, the gap between RG social classes I and V had actually increased.

■ Townsend and Phillimore in a study of health in the North East found similar trends and concluded that the health gap was the result of the wealth gap. Statistics published in the 1990s indicate that it is still a major problem.

hegemonic Marxism: see *structuralist Marxism.*

hegemonic masculinity: see *masculinity.*

hegemony: the domination, especially intellectually and culturally, of one social group, usually a social class, over another.

■ The term was developed by the Marxist Gramsci to explain why the political and cultural perceptions held by the working class generally consented to support the ruling class. He suggested that this was the result of powerful ideological apparatuses such as education and the media which socialised the mass of the working class into accepting the intellectual and moral leadership of the ruling elite as normal and natural.

■ *e.g.* According to some Marxist thinkers, working-class deviant youth *subcultures* have succeeded temporarily in challenging hegemony by appropriating and inverting traditional symbols such as the union jack to subvert and shock 'decent' society.

■ *TIP* Note that the concepts of *ideology, cultural capital* and hegemony are interconnected and form a crucial part of the Marxist theories of *stratification*, power, media and education.

heterogeneous group: a group that is socially mixed in that it has different characteristics, e.g. in terms of age, social class, gender, ethnicity, experience etc.

- *TIP* Contrast with *homogeneous group*.

hidden curriculum: the ways in which the organisation of teaching, knowledge and school regulations and routines shape pupil attitudes and behaviour in order to encourage *conformity*.

- It is usually contrasted with the formal curriculum, which is normally concerned with the teaching and testing of subject-based knowledge.
- *e.g.* Most sociological work on the hidden curriculum has focused on its allegedly negative consequences in promoting acceptance of inequalities relating to class, gender and ethnicity.
- *TIP* Marxist, feminist and *symbolic interactionist* theories of educational *underachievement* focus on the role of the hidden curriculum as a major cause of educational inequality.

hierarchies of credibility: an idea, originating with Becker, which argues that those in power are more likely to be consulted and have their version of truth accepted by agencies such as the mass media.

- *Critical sociologists* argue that news organisations are not as impartial as *pluralists* claim, because they often over-rely on an official version of events that reflects the interests of the powerful.
- *e.g.* Those who lack power may find their version is ignored, not taken seriously or defined as deviant. Becker argued that one of the roles of the sociologist was to give a voice to such 'outsiders'.

high culture: the culture of the *elite* or higher social classes.

- It is often distinguished from *mass* or *popular culture*, which is associated with the working class.
- *e.g.* High culture in the UK includes opera, classical music, Shakespeare, classical literature, poetry etc. Supporters of high culture believe it has artistic merit and aesthetic qualities that can only be appreciated with good breeding and the appropriate education.
- *TIP* See *cultural capital* and *habitus* for a Marxist perspective on high culture.

historical document: *secondary data* such as a government report, parish register, *census* records etc. produced in the recent or distant past which give insight into social phenomena, events and trends.

- John Scott notes that the *reliability* and *validity* of historical documents should be tested by asking key questions about the authenticity, credibility, *representativeness* and meaning of such documents.
- *e.g.* Both Laslett and Anderson were reliant on historical documents for their evidence regarding the historical evolution of family life.
- *TIP* Sociologists are likely to use such data in conjunction with other methods as part of a *case study* or *triangulation* approach to research.

historical method: see *comparative method*.

homogeneous group: any group which shares the same social or physical characteristics.

horizontal extended family: see *extended family*.

horizontal segregation: a type of occupational segregation by sex that allocates men and women into different types of work such as men into coal-mining, building etc. and women into routine clerical and domestic services.

household: a social group such as a family or a group of student friends sharing common residence.

■ *Postmodern* critics of traditional family sociologists prefer this concept because they argue it reflects the reality of modern societies, in which there is a diversity of personal and social relationships. Traditionalists argue that the concept of a household is too narrow and that the use of the *family* concept is more realistic as many households do not have the same intensity and commitment as family interactions.

housework: unpaid *domestic labour* mainly carried out by women, whether they are in paid work or not.

■ *Functionalists* argue that the unequal distribution of domestic labour is biologically inevitable whilst *liberal feminists* see it as the result of *gender role socialisation* and the *patriarchal ideology* that states a 'woman's place is in the home'. *Marxist feminists* see domestic labour as serving capitalist interests, whilst *radical feminists* claim that it arises naturally from patriarchal oppression and exploitation in the family. Empirical studies suggest that women are still over-whelmingly burdened with the responsibility for domestic labour even when in employment, despite functionalist claims of *egalitarian* marriage.

■ *e.g.* Studies of full-time housewives suggest high levels of *alienation* and stress and the possibility of mental illness.

human capital theory: the view that children are a resource and if society invests in their skills and knowledge in terms of educational spending and investment, there will be a return for society in terms of technological advancement and national economic output.

■ *Functionalist* sociologists and the *New Right* are keen on strong links between education and the economy.

■ *e.g.* The *new vocationalism* is human capital theory put into practice.

hybrid culture: the subscription to values and norms that may derive from a combination of cultures due to inter-marriage or because a second generation of an ethnic minority comes into regular and sustained contact with its peer group in the host population.

■ Johal's research (1998) on second and third generation British-Asians indicates the adoption of a hybrid culture in that they inherit an Asian identity and adopt a British one. He argues that this involves assuming a 'white mask' in order to interact with white peers at school or college, but they also highlight cultural difference, especially in terms of religion, when required.

■ *e.g.* Young Asians move between one cultural form and another depending on context and whether being British or Asian is appropriate in regard to the company that is being kept, choice of marriage partner, consumption of alcohol, meat etc.

hypodermic syringe approach: the view that children and impressionable young adults are injected with a fix of sex, violence and anti-social activity contained in media output, especially television and films, and consequently are prone to imitate deviant and criminal behaviour.

■ Despite the simplicity of this model, it has been tremendously influential on governments and tabloid media opinion, and has resulted in cinema, television and even music being subjected to intense critical scrutiny and even *censorship*. Sociological research into the effects of media is largely inconclusive, although most sociologists agree that audiences are more active and intelligent in their interpretation of media content than the hypodermic syringe approach suggests.

■ *TIP* See *media drip effect, media effects* and *reception analysis* for other angles to this debate.

hypothesis: an informed guess about what might be happening in regard to a natural or social phenomenon, based on previous research and observation, which can be tested in research.

■ Generally a hypothesis will speculate about the link between an *independent variable* and a *dependent variable* (i.e. cause and effect).

hypothetico-deductive approach: the name given to the logic of the research approach that *positivist* science is thought to employ.

■ It involves the development of a *hypothesis* based on observation, which is tested empirically through the collection of data in a systematic, *objective* and *reliable* way, either under laboratory conditions or in the field. If the hypothesis is not supported by the evidence, it is rejected or revised. If it is supported by the evidence, it forms the basis of *theory* from which law-like *generalisations* may be made.

■ *TIP* Critically contrast with Popper's theory of *falsification*.

iatrogenesis: a term associated with Illich, used in the sociology of health, which refers to disease, illness or disability caused by medical treatment.

■ Illich identified three types of iatrogenesis. Clinical iatrogenesis refers to damage to health caused by doctors through drug treatments, e.g. side effects, addiction etc., and mistakes in surgery. Social iatrogenesis refers to how control of our bodies has been taken over by an overly bureaucratic health system. One effect of this has been the medicalisation of pregnancy and childbirth, in that pregnant women are treated as patients with a medical problem rather than as experiencing a natural life event. Cultural iatrogenesis refers to attempts to use drugs and surgery to escape our natural selves in terms of body image and ageing, e.g. plastic surgery etc.

ideal pupil: a term used by *symbolic interactionist* sociologists to refer to a stereo-typical pupil who meets teacher expectations in terms of academic factors, e.g. intelligence, ability, effort, concentration etc. and non-academic factors, e.g. conformist behaviour, appearance, dress etc.

■ Interactionists argue that all pupils are judged and labelled by teachers in terms of their proximity to or distance from the ideal pupil stereotype.

■ *e.g. Critical sociologists* have suggested that the ideal pupil is white, male and middle-class. Ideal pupils are alleged to receive more positive teacher attention and treatment than pupils who fail to fulfil the ideal criteria.

ideal type: a concept, first used by Weber, to describe an abstract model made up of a set of exaggerated characteristics that can be used to make comparisons with the real world.

■ Weber's best-known ideal type is his model of *bureaucracy*.

■ *TIP* Do not confuse 'ideal' with 'desirable'.

identity: a concept used by sociologists to refer loosely to our sense of *self,* especially our subjective feelings about how others perceive and interpret our behaviour.

■ Most major sociological theories aim to explain the source of identity.

■ *e.g. Functionalists* see identity as the product of *socialisation* into *value consensus,* whilst Marxists see it as the product of class position and in some cases shaped by ruling class *ideology. Interpretivists* see identity as constructed through interaction with others.

TIP There is also evidence that identity is shaped by *gender, ethnicity, religion, nation* etc.

identity politics: a term used by *postmodernists* which suggests that identity is no longer shaped by traditional factors such as social class, gender and ethnicity but instead is expressed through personal relationships; shared experiences such as sexuality; lifestyle choices such as fashion; and *conspicuous consumption*.

Young people, in particular, are thought to be less likely to identify with grand themes such as class politics or feminism. Rather they are thought to be more amenable to single issues, which involve the potential for individual self-expression.

e.g. Sexuality and gay rights, environmentalism, *new age movements*, dance music etc.

TIP *New social movements* are seen to be the vehicle for the expression of identity politics.

ideological state apparatus (ISA): a Marxist term used to describe institutions such as education, the mass media, religion and the family, which are part of the *superstructure* of society.

The main function of these agencies is to transmit ruling class *ideology* to convince subordinate groups (e.g. the working class) that inequality is natural and normal, so ensuring their consent. When consent breaks down, *repressive state apparatuses*, e.g. the police and armed forces, may be used.

TIP Althusser argues that education is a key ideological apparatus because the *hidden curriculum* successfully transmits the message that society is *meritocratic*, despite evidence to the contrary.

ideology: a dominant set of ideas, usually aimed at justifying some inequality, transmitted by a powerful group to a subordinate group via agents of *socialisation* such as the family, education, religion and mass media.

Critical sociologists such as Marxists and feminists use the concept of ideology in explaining why inequalities continue to persist in modern societies.

e.g. Marxists see *ideological state apparatuses* as crucial to maintaining *capitalism*. They argue that ideology is so powerful that it results in the working class experiencing *false consciousness*. Feminists focus on *patriarchal ideology* to explain gender inequality in the workplace and in the home.

TIP Both Marxists and feminists have been criticised for their *over-deterministic* use of the concept.

illegitimacy: see *births outside marriage*.

illness: see *morbidity*.

immigration: the movement of people into a country or region on a permanent basis, usually for economic reasons.

Immigrants may have been pushed out of other countries or areas because of poverty, unemployment or political persecution. They are usually attracted to another country or area because of 'pull' attractions such as greater job opportunities, higher standards of living and greater political freedoms.

imperialism: the policy of acquiring and maintaining an empire, usually through the use of force.

■ It is particularly associated with the colonial expansion of the European powers, especially Great Britain in the eighteenth and nineteenth centuries.

■ *e.g. Dependency theory* suggests that British imperialism was responsible for the super-accumulation of wealth that financed the Industrial Revolution in Britain. Supporters of this theory note that the effects of imperialism are still being felt today through *neocolonialism.*

independent sector: see *private school.*

independent variable: a phenomenon or influence that is responsible for the presence of an effect (i.e. *dependent variable*).

■ In *experiments*, this is the characteristic being tested. It is often altered or manipulated during the research to determine whether it causes change in a situation.

index of deprivation: an attempt by Peter Townsend to operationalise the concept of *relative poverty* by constructing a list of 12 lifestyle characteristics that are either widely shared or approved of as necessary by a majority of society, e.g. diet, furnishings etc.

■ Townsend's estimates of poverty are based on the view that those in poverty are excluded from enjoying characteristics that most people take for granted.

■ *e.g.* The Breadline Britain survey of Mack and Lansley adopted a similar approach.

individualism: ways of thinking, usually subscribed to by Conservative and *New Right* thinkers, that focus on and emphasise the importance of the individual.

■ Such thinking views the notion of putting the group before the individual (i.e. collectivism) as an obstacle to social and economic efficiency because it supposedly undermines incentive, motivation and competition, which are viewed as essential tenets of capitalist enterprise.

■ *e.g.* The concept of individualism is central to *functionalist* and *New Right* theories of education and *modernisation theory.*

■ *TIP* Note too that Durkheim claimed that 'excessive individualism' resulted in *egoistic suicide.*

industrial conflict: conflict in the workplace between management and workers that is expressed through organised and usually formal action such as *strikes,* working to rule, and overtime bans, and informal action such as *industrial sabotage*, absenteeism, theft and resignation.

industrialisation: the general process in which societies and economies based on agricultural production evolve into societies and economies based on factory production, underpinned by science and technology and aimed at processing raw materials and/or the manufacture of goods.

■ Industrialisation in the West is mainly associated with *capitalism.*

■ *e.g.* In terms of *world sociology, modernisation theory* sees it as the ultimate goal of *development* whilst Marxists see it as accompanied by a range of social problems caused by its capitalist organisation, especially *social inequality.*

industrial relations: the study of the rules that govern relations between management and workers and which in the UK are mainly characterised by *collective bargaining* in which representatives of workers, i.e. trade unions, negotiate with employers.

■ Some sociologists, notably Dahrendorf, argue that industrial relations in Great Britain has institutionalised *class conflict*. Marxists, on the other hand, argue that industrial relations as expressed through collective bargaining merely channels conflict into safe issues that do not threaten capitalist interests and contribute to the *false consciousness* of workers.

industrial sabotage: the deliberate damage of machinery or products as a form of industrial action or protest.

■ Such behaviour may be a product of the *alienation* and *powerlessness* caused by modern management practices, e.g. assembly-line production.

■ *e.g.* Acts of sabotage could be interpreted as a type of worker resistance and protest and an attempt to re-assert control in an increasingly exploitative capitalist society, which denies workers power over the work process.

inequality: see *social inequality*.

infant mortality rate: the number of infants who die within 1 year of birth per 1,000 live births.

■ Infant mortality rates in the industrial West have declined quite dramatically since the beginning of the twentieth century. Infant mortality rates are often used as an indicator of *development* and a measurement of class and ethnic inequalities.

■ *e.g.* In the UK the working-class infant mortality rate is higher than those of higher-status groups.

informal economy: a type of economy that is made up of paid employment that is not declared to the authorities (i.e. the black economy) and unwaged work such as housework and work done for relatives, neighbours and friends such as babysitting, which is repaid in kind.

informal interview: see *unstructured interview*.

infrastructure (1): a Marxist term that describes the capitalist economic system, which is characterised by an unequal and exploitative relationship between the *bourgeoisie*, who own the *means of production*, and the *working class*, who hire out their labour in return for a wage.

■ The organisation of the infrastructure is therefore the root cause of inequality and the basis for great inequalities in wealth and income. Moreover, according to Marxists, the infrastructure exerts a great deal of influence over social institutions such as education, the mass media, religion etc., which make up the *superstructure* of society.

infrastructure (2): the system of institutions and services that make up the physical structure of a country, e.g. transport system, health service and schools.

■ Some sociologists believe that *development* can be measured by assessing whether a developing country has access to these institutions and services.

inner city: technically, the area that surrounds or exists alongside the central business district of most cities.

■ However, today sociologists use the term to describe all city areas that are characterised by social and economic deprivation, neglect and high crime rates, including those estates built on the outer edges of cities in the 1960s.

■ *e.g. Functionalist* theories of crime, e.g. the ecological theory of Shaw and McKay, suggested that the transitory nature of such areas, and their consequent lack of *community*, was responsible for the high crime rates seen there. The *New Right* suggests that the decline of the inner city has been caused by the emergence of a welfare-dependent and crime-committing *underclass*. However, *critical sociologists* have suggested that the deprivation associated with the inner city has been brought about by the mismanagement of capitalism.

institutionalisation: the effect of a long stay in an institution such as a mental hospital or prison, in which rules and regulations take control over the everyday activities of the inmate to the point that the inmate loses the ability to cope with life outside the institution.

■ Goffman's observations of life in a psychiatric hospital suggested that some inmates prefer life in the institution and resist attempts at rehabilitation. Goffman refers to this as colonisation.

■ *e.g.* One of the aims of the UK policy of *care in the community* was to avoid such over-dependency on institutions among patients.

institutional racism: the idea that racist assumptions are built into the rules and routines of social institutions such as the police, NHS etc., so neglecting the specific needs of *ethnic minority* groups and causing them disadvantage.

■ The McPherson Report into the death of Stephen Lawrence defined institutional racism as 'the collective failure of an organisation to provide an appropriate and professional service to people because of their colour, culture and ethnic origin'. Such *racism* is taken for granted and habitual — in other words, it has become so normal it is often not recognised as racism.

■ *e.g.* The practice of some police officers who automatically assume that black youths are suspicious or criminal.

instrumental collectivism: a term associated with the *affluent worker study*, carried out by Goldthorpe and Lockwood in the 1960s, to describe the attitude to work of manual workers working in prosperous areas in the southeast of England.

■ Goldthorpe and Lockwood noted that such workers defined work in instrumental ways, i.e. it was a means of earning money in order to improve their lifestyle rather than a source of identity. Moreover, such workers only took collective action to improve wages and lifestyle rather than out of any sense of working-class solidarity.

instrumentalism: a value system which focuses on adopting strategies, e.g. voting for a particular political party, membership of trade unions etc., that ensure the best possible economic and social return for the individual and their lifestyle.

■ Such values and behaviour reflect an *individualistic* outlook and generally contrast with values and behaviour that are motivated by *work satisfaction, altruism* and/or political allegiance and class loyalty.

instrumental leader: a term used by Parsons in his theory of the *nuclear family* and gender roles to describe the *masculine* role of breadwinner.

■ Parsons subscribed to the *biological determinist* view that males were genetically predisposed to be providers and protectors. He argues that for the family to function effectively there must be a *sexual division of labour* in which males and females occupy specific and distinct roles which complement each other and make equally important input into family stability. Feminists are extremely critical of this idea. They argue that such roles are socially constructed rather than biologically inherited through the process of *gender role socialisation*.

■ *TIP* Discussion of instrumental leaders should always include reference to *expressive leaders*.

instrumental Marxism: a theory of the media and the state, mainly associated with Ralph Miliband. It is also known as manipulative Marxism.

■ Miliband argues that the ownership and control of the mass media, especially newspapers, is in the hands of a capitalist *elite* who manipulate their content in order to reproduce, maintain and legitimate class inequality. Similarly, Miliband argues that the political elite, i.e. civil servants and politicians, are closely connected to the economic elite by kinship and marriage, education and business interests and consequently use the state as an instrument to preserve and protect the capitalist system.

■ *TIP* Miliband's ideas should be critically compared with *pluralist* theories of the media and the state and *structuralist Marxist* theory.

instrumental voting: voting behaviour, usually associated with working-class *instrumental collectivists*, that is motivated by obtaining the best financial return from the election of a particular political party in terms of taxation etc.

■ There is some evidence that Conservative election victories in the 1980s and 1990s may have been underpinned by such a working-class vote, especially in the southeast. These voters probably switched to Labour in 1997 after being persuaded that Labour would adopt prudent economic management policies.

intelligence: a contentious concept, it is usually defined as the capacity to reason in an abstract way and is measured by use of *IQ tests*.

■ Some sociologists, notably Saunders, have claimed inherited or innate intelligence is the cause of the educational underachievement and limited upward *social mobility* experienced by children of the working class and some ethnic minorities. However, some sociologists argue that intelligence takes a number of forms (abstract reasoning is only one type) and consequently IQ tests are problematical measures of intelligence.

■ *TIP* Social and environmental factors may be more important than innate intelligence in explaining social inequalities.

interactionist: see *symbolic interactionism*.

interest group: see *pressure group*.

intergenerational mobility: the movement of individuals up and down the class structure, measured by occupational status, compared with their parents, i.e. *social mobility* from one generation to the next.

■ *e.g.* Children from professional backgrounds were four times more likely to enter professional jobs than their working-class peers according to the *Oxford mobility study*.

intermediate class: a term used by John Goldthorpe as part of his model of social class which was based on seven broad occupational groups compressed into three social classes: the *service class*, the *intermediate class* and the *working class*.

■ Classification:

(1) Higher-grade professionals

(2) Lower-grade professionals

(3) Routine non-manual

(4) Small proprietors and self-employed

(5) Technicians and supervisors

(6) Skilled manual workers

(7) Semi- and unskilled manual workers

The intermediate class is composed of classes 3, 4 and 5. The Goldthorpe scale forms the basis of the *National Statistics Socioeconomic Classification (NS–SEC)* which replaced the *Registrar-General's classification of occupations* in 2000.

international division of labour: a system of international production in which different parts of a final product are made in different countries by *transnational companies*.

■ *e.g.* The technical parts may be manufactured in the West whilst the assembly of a product may be done in a low-waged *less developed country*.

interpretive/interpretivist sociology: an umbrella term for a group of *anti-positivist* theories including *symbolic interactionism* and phenomenology which suggest that the social world is socially constructed, i.e. a product of interaction and the meanings or interpretations that people bring to that interaction.

■ Interpretivists believe in adopting *ethnographic* research tools which emphasise *verstehen* and *validity* and which produce *qualitative data* that explore the interpretation of the world held by the research subjects.

■ *e.g.* Interpretivists stress the ability of individuals to exercise control and choices over their actions. The individual is seen not as a passive recipient of society's directions but as an active creator of social behaviour. The social world is a world of meaning because society is the outcome of shared interaction and interpretation.

■ *TIP* This theoretical perspective is especially important when discussing reasons why sociologists choose particular research strategies, and is often contrasted with *positivism*.

interview: an interaction between a sociologist and a respondent that may involve the working through of a standardised questionnaire or interview schedule (i.e. a *structured interview*), or an informal conversation which is loosely directed by an interviewer who plays a low-key role (i.e. the *unstructured interview*).

interviewer bias or effect: a methodological problem caused by the fact that interviews are interaction situations and may be affected by *status* differences between the interviewer and interviewee.

■ The status of the interviewer, e.g. their social class, age, gender and ethnicity, may be interpreted by the interviewee as threatening, patronising etc. and this may undermine the *validity* of the data collected.

■ *e.g.* Bias may also be caused by the interviewer's facial expression or tone of voice, leading the interviewee to a response that reflects the interviewer's own beliefs.

■ *TIP* Another variation on interviewer effect or bias is the *social desirability effect*.

interview schedule: a series of standardised questions which *operationalise* a particular *hypothesis* or research proposal and which are conveyed to a respondent during a *structured interview*.

■ Interview schedules are thought to be reliable by *positivist* sociologists, because any number of interviewers can replicate them. The status and personality of the interviewer should in theory have little impact on the data collected.

intragenerational mobility: movement between jobs and therefore social classes over the period of the lifetime of an individual, e.g. starting on the shopfloor and working up to company director.

■ *TIP* Note the difference between this and *intergenerational mobility*.

intrinsic satisfaction: the satisfaction derived from the experience of work, i.e. because the job involves creativity, autonomy, control and social interaction.

■ It is argued that jobs involving intrinsic satisfaction are in decline, especially in manual work, because managers have taken control of the organisation of work away from workers. It is argued by Goldthorpe and Lockwood that workers today are more motivated by extrinsic rewards, i.e. maintaining their family's standard of living etc.

introversionist sect: a type of religious sect which believes in cutting itself off from society because it perceives it to be immoral and a threat to its religious integrity.

■ *e.g.* Jim Jones' People's Temple retreated into the jungle of Guyana where its 800-plus members committed mass suicide.

inverse care law: the trend in NHS spending, first noted by Tudor Hart, that those areas in which health levels are good receive more resources in terms of number of hospital beds, doctors and nurses per head of population than areas in which poor health is the norm. The southeast therefore receives more resources than the northeast, despite the latter experiencing higher levels of *morbidity* and mortality.

■ The 'law' is not consistently true over all areas, e.g. Scotland has a poor record of health in terms of *mortality* and *morbidity rates*, yet it has consistently received a greater share of NHS resources than England. East Anglia, which enjoys relatively good levels of health, has traditionally had a low level of health spending relative to other English areas.

IQ: intelligence quotient, usually expressed as the formula:

$$IQ = \frac{mental\ age}{actual\ age} \times 100$$

■ The view that *intelligence* is hereditary, i.e. passed down from parents to children, was once very popular as an explanation of working-class educational *underachievement*.

■ *e.g.* Peter Saunders has recently suggested that genetic differences in terms of IQ are responsible for the superior educational attainment and *social mobility* experienced by children from middle-class backgrounds. A similar argument was employed by Eysenck and Jensen who suggested that black under-achievement was due to lower inherited IQs compared with white people.

IQism: a critical term used by the Marxists, Bowles and Gintis, to describe an ideology underpinning *meritocratic* education which argues that educational success is the result of inherited and superior *intelligence* that can be measured using IQ tests.

■ Bowles and Gintis argue that this ideology functions to disguise the true cause of educational inequality, i.e. socioeconomic background.

■ *e.g.* As Bowles and Gintis point out, even if IQ scores are accepted as measuring something, middle-class children with similar IQs to working-class children achieve considerably more educational and occupational success.

IQ tests: attempts to measure empirically the amount of *intelligence* a person has.

■ The *tripartite system* of education was based on the belief that intelligence was both inherited and measurable at the age of 11 by an IQ test (the *eleven-plus examination*). A child's test results determined whether he or she was allocated to a *grammar school*, for academic children, or a *secondary modern*, for the rest. Such tests are now generally thought to be unreliable because they are culturally biased in favour of middle-class white children whose social backgrounds made them more familiar with the sorts of question asked.

iron law of oligarchy: the view held by the classical *elite* theorist Robert Michels that power will always pass into the hands of an oligarchy (i.e. rule by a few), regardless of the best intentions of those committed to democracy or communist principles.

■ For Michels the problem is rooted in the need for governments, political parties and trade unions to have organisation. This is usually controlled by a small elite who monopolise expertise and communications and who come to enjoy the status and elite lifestyle that derives from this and that attracts the deference of others. This elite is therefore reluctant to give up or share power with others.

■ *e.g.* Michels argues that even working-class politicians come to resemble their *bourgeois* counterparts in terms of lifestyle and attempts to retain power.

isolated nuclear family: see *relative isolation of the family*.

job satisfaction: see *work satisfaction*.

joint conjugal roles: a concept, first used by Bott and developed by Wilmott and Young, that describes marriages characterised by the sharing of *housework* and childcare, decision-making and friendship networks.

■ This relationship forms the basis of Wilmott and Young's *symmetrical family* study in which they claimed that modern marriage was characterised by *equality* as expressed through women going out to work and men participating fully in housework and childcare.

■ *TIP* This idea has attracted a great deal of empirical research, especially by feminist sociologists who suggest that the idea of joint conjugal roles is exaggerated and women still carry the burden of domestic labour even when holding down full-time jobs.

juvenile delinquency: crime and deviant acts committed by young people.

■ Official criminal statistics suggest that crime is overwhelmingly committed by the 14–21 age group. The peak age for criminal offences is 18 years. Up to the 1970s sociologists developed theories that aimed specifically to explain the origins of delinquency in terms of young people's subscription to deviant *subcultures* or poor parental *socialisation*. However, today sociological theories tend to focus on deprivation and marginalisation (i.e. *left realism*) or the lack of controls in the lives of young people (i.e. the *New Right* and *control theory*).

■ *TIP* Most modern theories of crime can be applied to explaining juvenile delinquency because juveniles commit more crimes than adults.

kinship network: people related to each other by blood, marriage, *cohabitation* and adoption, who may be in frequent or infrequent contact with each other and who may feel a sense of obligation to each other, expressed in various forms of emotional, economic and social support.

■ There is sociological evidence that kinship networks act as a form of *mutual support system* in traditional working-class communities in which the *extended family* was the norm. However, some sociologists, notably *functionalists,* see such networks as less important in Western societies, which are characterised by the *relative isolation of the family.* However, recent evidence from sociologists such as Finch and Mason and Peter Willmott suggests that kinship networks still flourish in modern societies.

■ *TIP* There are a range of kinship types — see *local, dispersed* and *attenuated extended family.*

knowledge: a set of beliefs about what is 'true' and waiting to be discovered, taken-for-granted commonsense or ideological falsehoods, depending on the theoretical position adopted.

■ *e.g. Positivists* suggest knowledge is made up of objective scientific laws that exist independently of the sociologist and consequently are true in all places and at all times. *Interpretivist* sociologists argue that knowledge is socially constructed via interaction and interpretation and consequently includes everything people think is true, including commonsense, whether people can prove it or not. Moreover, it is not an objective reality. Rather, it is relative to specific societies and cultures. *Critical sociologists* argue that definitions of knowledge, especially in schools, are shaped by *bourgeois,* male and white Christian ideology, which devalues forms of knowledge associated with the working class, females and ethnic minorities in order to maintain inequality.

■ *TIP* Think about how Bourdieu's concept of *cultural capital* is essentially a critique of the ideological use of knowledge by the capitalist class.

labelling theory: a *symbolic interactionist* approach that focuses on the negative labelling of certain social groups as deviant by the *agents of social control*, e.g. teachers, police officers, the courts, the mass media etc.

■ Such *stereotyping* may result in those groups underachieving in education or becoming criminal statistics.

■ *e.g.* Interactionists like Becker argue that the stereotyped categorisation of subordinate groups by more powerful groups can lead to both *self-fulfilling prophecies* and deviant *subcultural* responses.

■ *TIP* Note that labelling theory has made an important contribution to the sociology of deviance because it was the first theory to draw attention to the role of power in defining what counts as deviance and to focus on the consequences of being labelled deviant.

laboratory experiment: see *experiment*.

labour market: the buying and selling of human labour power as a commodity.

■ Sociologists such as Barron and Norris, working within a Weberian tradition, argue that there are two distinct labour markets, i.e. *primary* and *secondary*, offering different sets of social rewards for different social groups. Marxists argue that the labour market is characterised by the exploitation of the labour of the working class by the capitalist class whilst other *critical sociologists* see the labour market discriminating against women and ethnic minorities.

labour power: a term that generally refers to the effort and industry expended by the working class in producing either raw materials or manufactured goods.

■ Marxists argue that *surplus value* is extracted from the labour power of workers and this is the basis of profit and therefore inequalities in wealth and power.

language code: particular type of verbal communication, such as *elaborated code* and *restricted code*.

■ Basil Bernstein claimed that particular language codes were associated with particular social classes and partly responsible for educational success and working-class *underachievement*.

latent function: an unintended function or consequence of a social institution as opposed to one that was intended, i.e. a *manifest function*.

■ *e.g.* The latent function of vocational training programmes might be to keep young people off the streets whilst the manifest function might be to equip them with skills to get jobs.

LDC: see *less developed country.*

league tables: a means of informing parents about how a school is performing compared with other schools introduced by the 1988 Education Reform Act.

■ A number of such tables are published giving information in regard to school performance in standardised assessment tests (SATs), GCSE and A-level as well as attendance and truancy rates. Critics of such tables believe them to be a very crude measure of a school's effectiveness.

■ *e.g.* Such tables do not take into consideration that the cause of a school's poor league table position might be the economic nature of a school's catchment area, such as high levels of economic and social deprivation. Critics of league tables believe that they create the potential for *sink schools*.

left idealism: see *new criminology*.

left realism: an analysis and explanation of street crime, particularly associated with Jock Young and John Lea, which states that working-class and ethnic minority crime are a real problem in inner-city areas.

■ Left realism is critical of attempts to show that the official criminal statistics merely reflect over-policing of working-class and ethnic minority communities.

■ *e.g.* Young and Lea argue that the statistics are probably a realistic reflection of crime committed by these groups; they point out that crime may be a rational response to feelings of *relative deprivation* and *marginalisation* experienced by younger members of the working class and some ethnic minorities.

■ *TIP* This is a crucial theory that has made an important contribution to sociological debate about the reliability and validity of *official statistics* on crime and of sociological explanations of crime.

left-wing: any set of political ideas that are critical of the status quo or which challenge *right-wing* political beliefs.

legal-rational organisations: any *organisation* that is characterised by a hierarchy of officials (i.e. *bureaucracy*) whose *authority* is accepted without question.

■ Weber saw bureaucracies as the *ideal type* of organisation and as having technical supremacy over all other types in terms of the efficient pursuit of organisational goals. Weber claimed such organisations have common characteristics.

■ *e.g.* Officials are recruited on the basis of ability and organised hierarchically in a chain of command. All responsibilities and duties are shaped by an inflexible set of rules and regulations, i.e. red tape, which are written down and regularly consulted.

legitimation: the process by which the mass of the population come to accept the rule of the few as natural and normal and consequently the organisation of society as just, despite the existence of inequalities in wealth and power.

- Marxists see such legitimation or rule by consent as the product of the activities of ideological state apparatuses such as education (i.e. the hidden curriculum) and mass media, which ensure the cultural hegemony of the capitalist class and therefore the false consciousness of subordinate groups such as the working class.
- **TIP** Stuart Hall's concept of *authoritarian populism* is a good illustration of legitimation in practice.

leisure: a concept defined as the time in which people are free from other social obligations, particularly work — a time of freedom, individual choice, self-expression and creativity.

- Our experience of leisure is shaped by factors such as social class, gender and ethnicity.

leisure class: a term coined by Veblen to describe an economic *elite* who do not work because they live off profits, rents, share dividends and inherited wealth.

- Such an elite spend most of their time engaged in *conspicuous consumption* in order to attract public attention and status.

leisure industry: the large entertainment, sport and leisure corporations that developed in the late twentieth century.

- According to *critical sociologists*, these industries have transformed leisure into a commodity, and consumers of leisure are exploited in a similar way to workers (see *commodification*). Moreover, it is believed that such companies create false leisure needs using intensive advertising.
- *e.g.* A small number of brewing companies control the majority of public houses and consequently the availability and price of alcoholic drinks.

leisure poor: the notion that some groups, such as those in *poverty*, lack the material resources to engage in leisure activities that the rest of society take for granted.

- It has also been used to describe some groups, e.g. women, who may lack the time to engage in leisure activities because of childcare responsibilities.

leisure rich: the notion that some groups, e.g. the *leisure class*, have both the material resources and time to engage in leisure activities.

leisure society: an idea, associated with theories of *postindustrial society*, that work is becoming less important and consequently leisure will be available to all because of changing work commitments.

less developed country (LDC): a country with relatively little or no manufacturing industry and which, on a range of indicators of development such as life expectancy, infant mortality, the distribution of wealth and income, literacy levels and *infrastructure*, lags behind the industrialised West.

- Such countries tend to be found in Africa, Asia and Latin America. *Modernisation theory* blames internal obstacles such as their culture for lack of development, whilst *dependency theory* suggests that their economies have been deliberately underdeveloped and exploited by the West.

liberal feminism: a feminist perspective that argues for equal rights for women and has consequently advocated legislation in order to prevent *discrimination* against women, especially in the workplace.

■ Liberal feminists see inequality between men and women as rooted in the *patriarchal* family and especially *gender role socialisation*.

■ *e.g.* They argue that conditioning into gender roles involves females being discouraged from realising their full potential. Other agencies of socialisation, particularly education and mass media, contribute to this process.

■ *TIP* Be aware that liberal feminists are generally optimistic about change and point to female achievement in education, the *feminisation of labour*, women's increasing rights within the family and more positive representations of women in the media as evidence that traditional inequalities are being challenged and are consequently in decline.

liberation theology: a set of ideas subscribed to by some Catholic priests in Latin America that combines elements of Christianity and Marxism and supports the active resistance of the poor against oppression and inequality.

■ It is often cited as evidence that religion can promote *social change* if all alternative means of possible reform have been blocked.

■ *e.g.* In Nicaragua, the dictator General Somoza banned all political opposition and regularly used terror tactics to coerce his people. Priests subscribing to liberation theology helped lead the Sandanista revolution, which overthrew him in 1979.

■ *TIP* The fact that liberation theology was disowned by the Catholic Church is useful in lending support to the Marxist view that the established church is an ideological tool of capitalist interests.

life chances: the opportunities or lack of opportunities to acquire material, social and cultural rewards, e.g. education, jobs, income, wealth, health, standard of living etc., that members of society can expect.

■ In a meritocracy, all social groups ideally experience the same opportunities. However, there is evidence that some social groups in the UK, e.g. the working class, ethnic minorities and women, do not have access to the same life chances as the upper and middle classes, whites and men respectively.

life cycle: predictable and significant events or stages that occur in the lives of most people.

■ Traditionally, the life cycle would generally be composed of the following stages: birth, childhood, adolescence, young adult (characterised by work and courtship), adult (characterised by work, marriage and children), middle age (characterised by work and children leaving home), old age (characterised by retirement) and death. However, this traditional pattern has been disrupted by longer periods spent in education, increasing divorce rates, *cohabitation*, *reconstituted families*, early retirement, changing definitions of women's roles etc. Diversity therefore increasingly characterises the life cycle.

life history: a sociological research method that includes an account of a particular historical period by an individual who lived through it.

■ Data are normally collected by *unstructured interviewing*, although they may also involve the analysis of *secondary data* such as letters, photographs and *diaries*. The method appeals to *interpretivist* sociologists, who believe in making sense of the past by accessing the interpretations of those living in the past. However, the data collected by this biographical approach may lack *validity* because recall might be distorted by bad memory and the tendency to over-romanticise the past. See also *oral history*.

linguistic deprivation: the view developed by Basil Bernstein and hijacked by *cultural deprivation theory* that the working class are disadvantaged because they do not have access to the *elaborated code* used by the middle class and used to convey knowledge in classrooms.

■ Bernstein argued that a cultural difference existed between the working class and middle class in terms of access to language codes. Both could converse in the *restricted code* but the working class were less likely to have access to the elaborated code, which put them at an educational disadvantage because schools were organised around middle-class values and language.

■ *TIP* A sophisticated account of this theory should always acknowledge that Bernstein has been misinterpreted by supporters of cultural deprivation theory. Like Bourdieu, he focused on cultural difference rather than cultural deficiency.

local extended family: kin who live separately from each other but choose to be in regular physical contact with each other.

local management of schools: a policy introduced as part of the *Education Reform Act (1988)* that increased the financial responsibilities of head teachers and governors by giving them direct control of 90% of their school budget.

■ The *New Right* rationale for this policy was twofold. First, such autonomy would increase diversity and choice as heads would decide to specialise in particular areas in order to attract more pupils. Second, it would encourage competition between schools because school budgets depend on the numbers on the school roll.

lone-parent families: see *one-parent families*.

longitudinal survey: research, usually based around *interviews* and sometimes *questionnaires*, that focuses on a particular group over a period of years in order to monitor how much change is taking place in their lives.

■ Such surveys produce in-depth data about the group or social trends over time. The research team has time to establish a relationship with the group, which may produce more valid data. However, this method can also be problematic.

■ *e.g.* It can be difficult to find samples and research teams committed to such long-term research. The sample may drop out, die, move away etc., which increases its chances of being unrepresentative. There is also a danger of a *social desirability effect*, as those being researched identify too closely with the research team, who themselves may experience the problem of *going native*.

looking-glass self: the idea, developed by Charles Cooley (1902), that a crucial part of *identity*, i.e. how people see themselves, is constructed by constantly checking how *self* is reflected in the responses of others.

■ *e.g.* A woman may see herself as a good sister because her siblings react positively to her in that role.

loss of community: a thesis which argues that communities in the past were warmer, friendlier and more supportive than those found today, especially those found in urban and inner-city areas.

■ The idea is rooted in Tönnies' ideas about *Gemeinschaft* and *Gesellschaft*.

■ *e.g.* Empirical studies such as Wilmott and Young's study of Bethnal Green do note a strong sense of community in the East End of London in the 1950s. However, it is argued that such communities have been either dismantled by slum clearance programmes and rehousing to new council estates or eroded by the problems associated with the decline of inner-city areas, such as crime.

■ *TIP* Be aware that the thesis may be based on a romanticised view of the past and that it also ignores the existence of *proto-communities*.

loss of family functions: a thesis associated with the *functionalist* thinker Talcott Parsons which suggests that the family in *preindustrial society* was a multi-functional *extended family*, responsible for production, education, health etc. but lost these functions at the onset of industrialisation to specialised agencies such as the factory system and the state.

■ Parsons argues that this process of *structural differentiation* left the family free to specialise in the *primary socialisation* of children and the *stabilisation of adult personality*. The thesis has been challenged both by historians and by feminists. Even sociologists sympathetic to functionalism such as Wilmott and Young and Ronald Fletcher note that the family still plays a significant role in the education, health, welfare etc. of its members.

low culture: see *mass culture, popular culture*.

macro-sociology: the study of social systems and how they are organised in terms of *social structure* and institutions.

■ Marxism takes a macro approach because it focuses on how the organisation of the economy in terms of class relationships influences the organisation of all other social institutions such as the educational system, political system etc. Functionalism also takes a macro approach because it focuses on how social institutions function to ensure *social order*. Macro theories rarely focus on individual behaviour.

■ *TIP* Always contrast this approach with *micro-sociology*.

magic bullet: see the *hypodermic syringe approach*.

maintained sector: the state-financed sector of the educational system, e.g. *comprehensive schools* at secondary level, as opposed to the fee-paying *private schools*.

male gaze: a concept used to describe why women's bodies are used in a decorative sexualised way to sell products in advertising and why women are generally portrayed as sex objects in films.

■ It is assumed by advertisers and other producers of media that economically affluent audiences are predominantly male and therefore the dominant audience interpretation will be from the male point of view.

malestream sociology: the feminist view that a great deal of sociology is dominated by male sociologists and therefore by *masculine* ways of looking at the world.

■ The sociology of *crime* and *deviance* and *social mobility* studies have particularly been accused of rendering females invisible.

male underachievement: the trend for males to underachieve in education relative to females.

■ Boys' underachievement has always existed but until the 1990s working-class boys used to move easily into jobs without good qualifications, such as factory jobs. Moreover, the structural and cultural barriers to girls' achievement in education and especially employment, e.g. male dominance of the professions and management and the emphasis on women becoming wives and mothers meant that males nearly always obtained better jobs than females. However, male underachievement has become an issue because of the decline in male employment and because large numbers of unemployed young men are seen as a threat to *social order*. Sociological explanations for male underachievement mainly focus on schools, parents and *gender role socialisation*.

■ *e.g.* Studies of classroom interaction and the relationship between pupils and teachers suggest that teachers have low expectations of boys and consequently a culture of low achievement has been allowed to evolve and prosper among boys. Other sociologists have suggested that children, both male and female, may equate learning with femininity because of their female primary school teachers and mothers. As young males become more aware of their masculinity they may reject learning because of its feminine connotations. Mac An Ghaill argues that working-class boys are experiencing a *crisis of masculinity* as their perception of what a man is and how he ought to behave has been undermined by unemployment and the feminisation of work. This confusion about future roles as men may lead working-class boys to conclude that qualifications are a waste of time because there are only limited opportunities in the job market.

■ *TIP* Male underachievement is important but the new emphasis on it in textbooks does not mean that *female underachievement* has been resolved.

managerial revolution: a phrase coined by Burnham to describe the rise of a managerial class who control and manage companies on behalf of owners in return for high rewards.

■ The idea of a managerial revolution has been used by sociologists such as Dahrendorf to suggest that there has been a split between ownership and control.

■ *e.g.* According to both Burnham and Dahrendorf, owners no longer exert control over companies. Rather, power is widely dispersed amongst share-holders, who appoint directors, and managers, who take professional and objective responsibility for the day-to-day policy-making and administration of companies.

■ *TIP* Contrast this with the Marxist view that owners still exercise considerable power because shares are often concentrated in few hands.

manifest function: the intended function of a social institution, such as the transmission of knowledge in education.

manipulative Marxism: see *instrumental Marxism*.

manual work: physical labour carried out by manual or *blue-collar workers* and defined as a characteristic of working-class occupations.

■ Manual work is in decline in the UK.

■ *e.g.* University lecturers outnumber miners in the UK.

marginalisation: a concept referring to the *powerlessness* of particular social groups, e.g. the working class, the young and ethnic minorities, to overcome social and economic inequalities and/or injustices that they may experience.

■ The *left realists* Young and Lea suggest that the frustration experienced by working-class and ethnic minority youth that leads to crime and inner-city

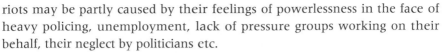

riots may be partly caused by their feelings of powerlessness in the face of heavy policing, unemployment, lack of pressure groups working on their behalf, their neglect by politicians etc.

marital breakdown: an umbrella term that encompasses divorce, separation and *empty-shell marriages.*

■ Whilst it is relatively easy for sociologists to measure divorce, it is difficult to estimate accurately the true rate of marital breakdown.

■ *e.g.* Many people separate and don't divorce or legally register their separation. The true number of empty-shell marriages is impossible to estimate because of the private nature of family life in the UK. The accessibility of divorce has made such marriages less likely, although in some religious communities empty-shell marriages may be a lesser evil because divorce is frowned upon.

market conditions: a concept referring to the skills workers have to sell in the labour market, relative to other workers, which shapes their economic position in terms of size of income, degree of job security and promotion opportunities.

■ This concept has been adopted by the *NS–SEC* classification of occupations and social class introduced in 2000.

■ *e.g.* The NS–SEC occupational classification is partly based on market conditions which include things such as salary, promotion prospects, sick pay, pension, fringe benefits, how much control people have over the hours they work or how much work is done etc.

■ *TIP* Know the NS–SEC well and why it has replaced the *Registrar-General's classification of occupations.*

market forces: the mechanisms of supply and demand that are part and parcel of the capitalist economic system in which buyers and sellers pursue their own interests without interference from agencies such as government within a competitive framework.

market research: research, usually in the form of *questionnaires* and *structured interviews*, carried out by professional polling organisations such as MORI, Gallup etc. or by advertising agencies using *quota sampling* to investigate consumption patterns or behaviour such as voting etc.

marriage: a legally ratified union between a man and a woman, although in some countries, e.g. the Netherlands, it is now legally possible for people of the same sex to be married.

■ Sociologists have noted declining rates of marriage in the UK. *New Right* sociologists see this trend as a symptom of both moral decline and family life being under attack. However, the evidence contradicts the New Right position.

■ *e.g.* Surveys indicate that most people see marriage as a desirable objective. People are probably delaying marriage until later in life after experiencing a period of *cohabitation* rather than rejecting it altogether. Moreover, *remarriage* now makes up one third of all marriages, which indicates that people are committed to the institution of marriage despite their previous negative experiences of it.

m

■ *TIP* Note that questions on marriage could also involve an examination of *conjugal roles, emotion work, divorce* and *domestic violence*.

Marxism: an influential *structuralist* theory, based on the works of Karl Marx, that sees capitalist societies as characterised by class inequality, exploitation and conflict.

■ Marxists focus on the economic relationships that underpin *capitalism* found in the *infrastructure* and argue that the *bourgeoisie* who own the *means of production* systematically exploit the *labour power* of the working class by extracting *surplus value*. This allegedly leads to great profits and consequently inequalities in wealth and power. Modern Marxists like Althusser, Bourdieu, Bowles and Gintis, Braverman and Miliband have made crucial contributions to the study of *stratification*, education, mass media, work, the *state* etc.

■ *e.g.* Modern Marxists have focused on the role of social institutions as part of the *superstructure* in transmitting ruling-class *ideology*, which allegedly encourages *false consciousness* and reproduces, maintains and legitimates class inequality as a 'natural' feature of capitalism.

■ *TIP* Be aware of disagreements between different schools of Marxism and the fact that Marxism in general is criticised for its *over-determinism*, its *economic reductionism* and its neglect of other possible sources of inequality such as gender and ethnicity.

Marxist feminism: a feminist perspective which sees gender inequalities as a product of *capitalism*.

■ It is argued that women occupy a more subordinate position than men in terms of the class relationships that characterise the *infrastructure* for four broad reasons:

(1) They generally earn less than men in paid employment, are less likely to be found in professional and managerial posts and are more likely to be found in part-time work.

(2) Their responsibility for *domestic labour* ensures that the male workforce is fit and healthy.

(3) They reproduce and rear the future workforce free of charge.

(4) They may soak up the frustrations associated with male powerlessness in the workplace in the form of *domestic violence* which might otherwise be directed at the capitalist system.

Like Marxism, Marxist feminists are criticised for being *over-deterministic*, but also for neglecting the power of women to resist these processes and to make rational choices about their futures as mother-housewives.

masculinity: a set of social and cultural expectations mainly shaped or constructed during *gender role socialisation*.

■ Bob Connell notes that there are many different ways of being masculine.

■ *e.g.* He refers to traditional definitions of masculinity, such as being a breadwinner, head of household, dominant over women, a 'real' man etc., as 'hegemonic masculinity'. This is the dominant form of masculinity in society.

However, he also notes 'complicit masculinity' in which men may be more sensitive to women's needs and involved in child-rearing but still gain from a 'patriarchal dividend' in that men dominate the labour market and women are still overwhelmingly responsible for domestic labour. Connell refers to homosexuality as a form of 'subordinated masculinity', because it is still generally regarded as deviant.

■ *TIP* The mass media have championed the *new man*, in touch with his feminine side, but be aware that there is little evidence for his existence.

mass culture: the idea, mainly associated with the Marxist *Frankfurt School*, that the mass media are responsible for a commercialised *popular culture*, which revolves around superficial entertainment.

■ Marcuse saw such mass culture as an *ideology* that served to disguise the true extent of class inequality and exploitation and functioned to bring about *false needs* and *false consciousness* amongst the working class. It is argued that mass culture stifles creativity, imagination and critical thought in society.

■ *TIP* Don't assume such an effect upon the audience actually exists — it is impossible to prove.

mass media: forms of communication that transmit information, education, news and entertainment to mass audiences through instruments such as newspapers, magazines, advertising, radio, television, cinema, music and the internet.

■ There are basically four major sociological debates regarding the mass media in the UK. First, is media content determined by the audience, as *pluralists* argue, or shaped by capitalist interests, as Marxists argue? Second, does media content, especially sex and violence, cause copy-cat behaviour in young impressionable audiences? Third, are the media responsible for the 'dumbing down' of culture? Finally, do the media stereotype minority groups and consequently contribute to their subordinate position in society?

mass media reports: *secondary data* in the form of newspaper and magazine articles, television programmes, advertisements and films.

■ In particular, *interpretivist* sociologists have used mass newspaper reports to give insight into past events and social concerns. The sociology of *moral panic* is one such area.

■ *e.g.* Stanley Cohen analysed newspaper coverage of bank holiday disturbances in the mid-1960s involving mods and rockers in order to gain insight into how society defines social problems. Other sociologists are interested in how the media represent and stereotype social groups such as females and ethnic minorities. *Critical sociologists* such as the *Glasgow University Media Group* have studied media content, especially television news, for its ideological or political content, to see whether it supports ruling-class interests.

■ *TIP* The content of the mass media is normally researched using *content analysis* and/or *semiology*. It is important to have a clear idea of how these methods work in practice.

master status: a *symbolic interactionist* concept that refers to how a deviant label or status, e.g. 'criminal', may dominate all other statuses a person may have, e.g. son, husband, and consequently shape negative societal reaction to that person.

■ The label of criminal, for example, may prevent a person from joining in with 'normal' society, e.g. getting a job etc. This may lead to a *self-fulfilling prophecy* as the individual seeks *subcultures* of people with similar status and lives up to the master status.

material deprivation: an explanation for inequality and disadvantage in fields such as education and health and illness which focuses on the lack of material factors such as income and housing.

■ This explanation sees educational failure etc. as caused by influences such as global recession, *racism* etc. that are beyond the control of the individual.

■ *e.g.* Halsey and Floud note that working-class 16-year-olds with the same IQ and exam results as middle-class 16-year-olds are more likely to leave school because of poverty. Prosser identified a *cycle of deprivation*, which results in working-class children falling behind in skills such as reading and writing at a very young age.

■ *TIP* It is useful to see material deprivation as a critique of *cultural deprivation theory*, in that cultural values do not exist in a vacuum but are shaped by the material environment, e.g. poverty.

maternal deprivation: a theory associated with the psychologist John Bowlby, and extremely popular in the 1950s and 1960s, which argues that if the mother–child bond is interrupted for any given period of time the child may grow up to be emotionally and psychologically maladjusted.

■ Maternal deprivation is still immensely powerful and influential today and probably is still the main rationale for women taking long periods out of work to look after children and for the guilt experienced by many working women with young children.

matriarchy: a society or social group in which power is in the hands of females.

■ Such societies and groups are very rare, although studies of African-Caribbean families, one-parent families and some working-class extended families suggest it is the norm in these types of family.

■ *e.g.* Wilmott and Young's Bethnal Green study does offer evidence of matriarchal control, although most societies tend to be *patriarchal*.

matrilineal: descent or inheritance of titles, property etc. through the female line.

McDonaldisation: the process by which the principles of the McDonald's fast-food restaurants are coming to dominate global production and consumption across both the manufacturing and service sectors.

■ Ritzer notes that the company uses rational methods in order to ensure the uniformity of product and environment in which the product is consumed. He also notes that the *rationalisation* of production employed by McDonald's, and especially its employment of young low-paid and low-skilled workers, is becoming a global norm. Many companies are now adopting the policy of employing young people and women in low-skilled, low-paid, high-stress, exhausting, insecure jobs with little opportunity for promotion. Commentators like Ritzer and Naomi Klein refer to this trend as 'McJobs' in the 'McWork' sector.

meaning: a concept employed by *interpretivists* to describe the sum total of the interpretations and *commonsense knowledge* that people use to make sense of the social world and their interactions within it.

meaninglessness: an indicator of *alienation* identified by Blauner which refers to workers failing to feel a sense of pride, purpose or ownership in their work.

Blauner argued that assembly-line production was experienced by workers in this way and so workers found it difficult to identify with the product.

means of production: a Marxist concept that refers to the capital, land, factories, science and technology, i.e. machines, and raw materials, owned by the *bourgeoisie*.

means-tested benefit: a *selective benefit* that is only paid when the applicant has been assessed on the basis of need as opposed to a universal benefit, which is available to all citizens by right.

New Right thinkers on welfare see universal benefits as promoting *welfare dependency* and would prefer to see their replacement with more means-tested benefits. There has been a trend in recent years towards such benefits. However, there is evidence that means-testing is overly bureaucratic, complex and may put people off claiming benefits to which they are entitled.

mechanical solidarity: a concept invented by Durkheim referring to traditional, usually preindustrial societies in which *community* is more important than the individual.

Durkheim identified a number of features of societies characterised by mechanical solidarity.

e.g. The sharing of common beliefs, values and lifestyles and a simple division of labour in which members of society share the same skills etc. In these societies people feel a strong sense of obligation and commitment to the wider social group.

TIP Durkheim saw these societies as in decline and noted that *industrialisation* and *urbanisation* led to the development of more *individualistic* societies based on *organic solidarity*. See also Tönnies on *Gemeinschaft* and *Gesellschaft*.

media drip effect: a theory of *media effects* which argues that exposure to constant violence over the long term, especially in the socialisation years, results in a 'drip' effect in that children gradually come to see violence and aggressive behaviour as an acceptable problem-solving device.

This approach is a variation on the *hypodermic syringe approach* and is mainly associated with Elizabeth Newson, who argues that some children from deprived backgrounds are more likely to be exposed to such effects because they have uncontrolled access to television and videos.

media effects: a collection of theories which suggest that the media may have some sort of effect, whether positive or negative, on their audiences.

■ The *hypodermic syringe approach* and *media drip* model focus on the negative effect of media content, as do some feminist commentators who are convinced of the link between pornography and rape. Marxists have speculated about the 'dumbing down' and commercialisation of media content and its effect upon the working class. Other theories, particularly the social filters approach of Klapper, the *uses and gratifications* model and *reception analysis*, focus on how audiences use the media rather than how the media affect the audience.

media industries: refers to media organisations and their mass production of cultural goods such as films, television programmes, newspapers, magazines and music for global consumption in order to maximise market potential and profit.

■ *Postmodern* sociologists in particular have focused on how media products and audiences are marketed as commodities (see *commodification*).

■ *e.g.* Media industries see their consumers in terms of niche markets and lifestyle choices and consequently cultural products are manufactured with particular audiences in mind, e.g. 'slasher' movies for teen audiences, pop groups like Hear'say for *young adolescents* etc.

media reports: see *mass media reports*.

media representation: the way in which social groups are portrayed by the media.

■ Numerous sociological studies suggest that women, ethnic minorities, the disabled, young people and the elderly are portrayed by a range of media in a negative and prejudiced fashion, which may confirm their subordinate status in society.

■ *e.g.* In relation to females, concern has been expressed about a possible link between the representation of women's bodies and eating disorders.

■ *TIP* Don't make the mistake of assuming such effects exist — it is very difficult to 'prove' that such representations have an effect upon the audience or the group stereotyped.

medical model of health: see *biomechanical model of health*.

mental illness: any disorder that has an effect upon the personality and behaviour of an individual and is interpreted as preventing them from functioning adequately and/or as posing a threat.

■ Sociologists accept that some mental illness is physiological in origin but suggest that definitions of what counts as mentally ill behaviour may be socially constructed by powerful groups in order to control non-conformist behaviour.

■ *e.g.* Supporters of *labelling theory* claim that what counts as mental illness is a matter of interpretation and relative to particular cultures and historical periods. In particular, they argue that it is a means of controlling objectionable behaviour, e.g. in the former Soviet Union, political dissent was defined as a symptom of mental illness.

meritocracy/meritocratic: a type of society in which intelligence, ability and effort, i.e. merit, are rewarded through an *achievement*-orientated and *universalistic* education system.

■ Western societies are thought by *functionalist* sociologists to be characterised by an occupational system that allocates jobs and financial rewards purely on the basis of talent and skill. However, *critical sociologists* are sceptical about this claim.

■ *e.g.* Critical sociologists point to class, gender and ethnic inequalities in educational achievement, employment opportunities, pay, unemployment and social mobility as overwhelming evidence that meritocracy is a myth. Marxists, in particular, view the concept as an *ideology* aimed at convincing the working class that capitalist societies are fair and that any failure must therefore be self-inflicted.

metanarrative: a *postmodernist* term that describes those sociological theories such as functionalism and Marxism that aim to explore how modern societies work and that lay claim to being hard scientific truths in the process.

■ Postmodernists argue that such 'big stories' are no longer relevant in the postmodern world, which is characterised by a media explosion that has led to a fragmented social world characterised by greater choice and diversity.

■ *e.g.* Postmodernists argue that no one theory or metanarrative is able to explain such a world. However, postmodernism has been criticised for being a metanarrative itself.

methodological pluralism: the use by researchers of more than one method of research in order to build up a fuller and more comprehensive picture of social life.

■ By using more than one research method, the sociologist can enjoy the distinct advantage of each method and of the different kinds of data each produces.

■ *e.g.* The advantages of one method may help to compensate for and partially overcome the limitations of another.

■ *TIP* Do not confuse *triangulation* with methodological pluralism.

methodology: the sociological study of how sociological claims to knowledge are validated by the examination of the research methods used to gather and interpret data.

■ This study has been dominated by *positivist* and *interpretivist* approaches, although the 1980s and 1990s have seen sociologists abandoning slavish devotion to either positivist or interpretivist research methods.

■ *e.g.* Such sociologists have taken a pragmatic response and used a combination of *quantitative* and *qualitative* methods. For these sociologists, 'what works best is best'. Many sociological studies have used a combination of *primary* and *secondary* research methods in order to produce a quantitative and qualitative picture of a social phenomenon or problem.

■ *TIP* It can be argued that the degree of allegiance to either a positivist or an interpretivist approach was probably exaggerated by most sociology textbooks.

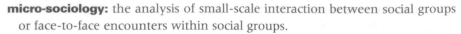

micro-sociology: the analysis of small-scale interaction between social groups or face-to-face encounters within social groups.

■ It is normally associated with *interpretivist sociology*, which is interested in interaction and the meanings that people bring to such social encounters.

■ *e.g.* This approach generally sees society as socially constructed as opposed to the *macro-sociology* approach, which sees society as existing independently of individuals and exerting an external influence upon their behaviour.

middle class: the socioeconomic group which is situated between the upper class and the working class, categorised by the *NS–SEC* as social class 1 (higher managerial and professional) and 2 (lower managerial and professional).

■ The middle class now constitutes the largest class in UK society. However, sociologists acknowledge distinct differences in market and work situations between different social groups within this broad category.

■ *e.g.* Savage notes the existence of six middle-class *class fractions* — higher and lower professionals, senior and middle managers, the self-employed and *white-collar workers*. Marxists argue that white-collar workers can no longer be regarded as middle-class because the *deskilling* of clerical work and the introduction of computer technology mean they have experienced *proletarianisation*.

migration: the movement of people from one country or region to another.

■ The total amount of migration in a society is usually estimated by comparing *immigration* with *emigration*.

millenarian movements: *sects* and *cults* that subscribe to apocalyptic beliefs that disasters and cataclysmic changes, usually predicted by either religious writing such as the Bible or charismatic leaders, will occur in the near future and will result in the transformation of old societies into a new moral beginning.

minority group: a social group which is outnumbered by other social groups and which may find itself allocated to subordinate and oppressed social positions because its distinct physical and cultural characteristics are interpreted as inferior, deviant etc. by the majority culture.

mixed economy: economies, such as the UK economy, that are subjected to free-market forces, i.e. competition, yet are also partly managed by the state, e.g. anti-inflationary policies.

MNC: see *multinational company*.

mode of production: a Marxist term describing how goods are produced in a society.

■ The mode of production in the West is *capitalist*. This involves a specific type of production.

■ *e.g.* The capitalist mode of production is based on factory-based technology and management control of the whole production process. It is also composed of specific reationships between employers and employees, i.e. Marxists believe that the *surplus value* of the labour of the *proletariat* is appropriated and exploited by the capitalist class. Therefore the mode of production is underpinned by class-based inequalities.

m

modernisation: a model of social *development* that, according to *modernisation theory*, should be aspired to by *less developed countries* and that involves *industrialisation* and the adoption of Western values, institutions and lifestyles.
■ Some sociologists suggest this concept is problematical because it is both loaded and *ethnocentric.*
■ *e.g.* It assumes Westernisation is the only worthwhile and desirable direction development should take. However, some societies may interpret modernisation as freedom from oppression or as the reduction of inequalities in wealth and power. Some societies have returned to traditional values, e.g. Islamic societies, which Westerners may regard as a backward step.

modernisation theory: a theory of development largely based on the view that to develop means to become 'modern' by adopting Western cultural values and social institutions.
■ The theory suggests that lack of development is caused by internal obstacles such as deficient cultural values and inefficient social institutions, which are unsuitable for the modern world.
■ *e.g.* Modernisation theory argues that countries require an injection of official *aid* and investment from *multinational companies* in the West in order to develop effectively. However, the theory has been criticised for being *ethnocentric,* for ignoring the social problems associated with capitalism, e.g. crime, poverty etc., and for underestimating exploitation by Western countries of the resources, labour and economies of *less developed countries.*
■ *TIP* Compare and contrast this perspective with *dependency theory.*

modernity: a term used to describe the modern world, which is generally seen as beginning with industrial production and characterised by urbanisation, the growth of the bureaucratic state and the widespread acceptance of rational scientific thinking.
■ Many of the classical sociological theories, especially functionalism and Marxism, aimed to explain *social change,* i.e. why modern societies had come about, and to describe and analyse their organisation. *Postmodernist* thinkers, however, argue that modernity is obsolete and that society has progressed into a postmodern age.
■ *TIP* Be aware of the distinction between modernity and postmodernity, and how this debate impacts on areas such as the mass media, the family etc.

modified extended family: a term coined by Litwak, who argues that despite geographical distance and social mobility, *nuclear families* still retain strong *affective relationships,* with extended *kinship networks,* especially grandparents, via telephone, e-mail, letters and visits.

monogamy: traditionally and legally, the practice of marriage between a woman and a man at any one time.
■ In modern societies its meaning has been widened by sociologists to focus on any long-term relationships, e.g. *marriage, cohabitation,* same-sex couples etc. characterised by sexual exclusivity and fidelity.

■ *e.g.* High rates of divorce and remarriage have led some sociologists to conclude that *serial monogamy* now characterises relationships in the UK.

moral entrepreneurs: powerful and vocal individuals and groups who are able to influence and shape public opinion as to what constitutes immoral and deviant behaviour.

■ Politicians, church leaders, editors of national newspapers and leaders of moral campaign groups such as the National Viewers and Listeners Association are all examples of moral entrepreneurs who are particularly vocal during *moral panics*.

moral panic: a concept first used by Jock Young and developed by Stan Cohen that refers to the media's ability to transform an event or social group into a threat to society (i.e. a *folk devil*) through sensationalist and stereotyped reporting of news.

■ The major characteristics of a moral panic are awareness of a potential threat (concern), clear divisions between 'them' and 'us' (hostility), strong agreement about the threat that is usually managed by *moral entrepreneurs* (consensus), over-anxiety about the perceived threat (disproportionality) and intense but short-lived reaction (volatility). Moral panics usually result in official crackdowns, e.g. more policing, tougher laws etc., which may have a *deviancy amplification* effect upon the *official statistics* on crime.

■ *e.g.* Moral panics in the UK have tended to focus on deviant youth *subcultures* (e.g. mods and rockers, punks etc.), drugs (e.g. heroin and ecstasy), satanic child abuse, one-parent families etc.

■ *TIP* Be aware of sociological explanations as to why moral panics occur.

moral regulation: a *functionalist* idea suggesting that a function of social institutions like the family, religion and the law is to ensure that members of society are socialised into a set of moral guidelines which shape social behaviour and continue to reinforce that behaviour during their lifetime.

■ Durkheim suggested that lack of such moral regulation might lead to individuals committing *anomic suicide,* whilst too much moral regulation could lead to *fatalistic* forms of suicide.

morbidity: illness and disease.

■ Friedson notes that doctors use objective medical knowledge to define what counts as illness in modern societies, which makes them very powerful *agents of social control*. However, according to *interpretivists*, it is impossible to define and measure morbidity because illness is a subjective state.

■ *e.g.* People may have a disease without feeling ill. People's sense of being well or unwell is relative, in that symptoms interpreted as illness by one person may be interpreted by another as part of the way he or she normally feels.

morbidity rate: the incidence of a specific disease or disorder calculated as the rate per 100,000 of the population in 1 year.

■ Such statistics show that some social groups, i.e. the semi-skilled and unskilled and some ethnic minority groups, experience a disproportionate share of diseases such as cancer and heart disease. The morbidity rate for most diseases has fallen nationally across all social groups, but the morbidity gap between professional and managerial groups and the unskilled has actually increased. However, morbidity statistics may be problematical because they are based on visits to GPs, hospital admissions etc.

■ *e.g.* The subjective and relative nature of morbidity means that statistics are only collected once the individual recognises he or she is ill.

mortality rate: the death rate measured by the number of deaths per thousand people in a population in a year.

■ The mortality rate in the UK has fallen considerably over the past 100 years. However, there are significant social class differences existing today between professionals and unskilled manual workers in terms of the mortality rate, which have actually increased in the last decade. There is a sociological debate between the *biomechanical* and *social models of health* in regard to the decline of the mortality rate in the twentieth century.

■ *e.g.* The biomechanical model argues that modern medical techniques such as vaccination, surgery etc. were responsible for the decline in the mortality rate. However, the social model suggests that the major influences were probably the introduction of public health schemes, i.e. sewage and clean water systems, improvements in diet and therefore nutrition, better housing and birth limitation.

mortification of self: a term invented by Erving Goffman to describe the process allegedly found in some *total institutions*, especially psychiatric hospitals, in which a person's identity is stripped of its unique characteristics and replaced by an identity and role imposed by institutional rules.

■ On entry to a total institution, Goffman's research indicated that a person is subjected to humiliating rituals, e.g. strip-searching, invasion of privacy and constant surveillance. Institutionalised life involves learning to conform to the institution's rules. Goffman argues that people respond in a variety of ways to this treatment.

■ *e.g.* In an institution some withdraw and become introverted. Some cooperate whilst others become dependent and experience *institutionalisation*. Some rebel whilst others 'play it cool', i.e. largely conforming but hanging on to some vestige of their old identity.

multiculturalism: the promotion of cultural diversity, which may be expressed by acknowledging and celebrating aspects of ethnic minority culture in, for example, education, and positively addressing problems that create inequality, e.g. access to employment.

multilateral aid: see *aid*.

multinational company (MNC): a corporation that has an American, European or Japanese base but has global interests in terms of extracting and processing raw materials and cash crops and/or producing and marketing manufactured goods across a range of countries, especially *less developed countries*.

■ *Modernisation theory* views MNCs positively and suggests that they play a crucial role in *development*. However, *dependency theory* argues that MNCs invest in the developing world because it provides cheap labour and raw materials and because marketplaces are potentially very profitable. The growth of MNCs is viewed by Marxists as an important feature of *neocolonialism*.

■ *e.g.* It was estimated in 1976 that about 400 MNCs control about one third of the fixed assets of the entire world. They therefore have great economic and political strength.

■ *TIP* Note the distinction between MNCs and *transnational companies*.

multistage sampling: a type of sampling method in which one *sample* is drawn from another sample or set of samples.

■ The most common practice is randomly to choose an area (e.g. region, city, town etc.) and randomly to select a sub-sample (e.g. district, constituency, schools etc.). A further random sub-sample might identify a couple of streets or year groups within specific schools which could then be targeted with *questionnaires*. This is a useful sampling method to use when no *sampling frame* is available. A map of the area acts as an alternative.

mutual support system: a network of material and emotional supports offered by a group to its members.

■ It was thought to be a major characteristic of the *proletarian traditionalist* working-class *extended family*.

■ *e.g.* Wilmott and Young's classic sociological study 'Family and kinship in East London' (1957) documented the material help that fathers provided for sons and mothers provided for daughters.

nanny state: a negative term used by *New Right* sociologists to suggest that the *welfare state* has created *welfare dependency* and disincentives to work, and consequently discourages individual responsibility.

nation: cultural communities made up of individuals who do not know each other or interact regularly but who are united by shared culture, history, language, rituals etc. in expressing a sense of *national identity*.

national curriculum: a standardised and formal curriculum, focusing on traditional academic knowledge and skills, that prescribes what should be taught in all state schools.

■ This curriculum, introduced by the *Education Reform Act (1988)* and accompanied by national assessment tests (SATs) at the ages of 7, 11 and 14, was the first state attempt to control the content of education across all schools. *New Right* sociologists see it as an attempt to raise standards, to increase efficiency and to link education more firmly to the needs of the economy through its emphasis on science and information technology. Marxists, however, see it as an integral part of the *hidden curriculum* which sees some types of knowledge, e.g. history, as transmitting the right sorts of *ideological* message whilst excluding critical subjects such as sociology, politics etc.

national identity: the feeling of being part of a larger community in the form of a *nation*, which gives a sense of purpose and meaning to people's lives as well as a sense of belonging.

■ It depends on the promotion of a common national culture through education, dress, diet, sport, national rituals and mass media. Anderson argues that national identity is socially constructed in the same way as gender or ethnic identity. Some sociologists suggest national identity may be under threat from *globalisation*.

nationalisation: a social policy particularly associated with the Labour government in power between 1945 and 1952 which involved taking economic resources such as railways and coal into public ownership.

■ Nationalisation was motivated by the view that certain industries were backward and inefficient and public ownership could redevelop these industries into more effective and modern organisations.

■ *TIP* Contrast with *privatisation*.

n

nationalism: a set of political beliefs and symbols, e.g. flags, expressing a sense of *identity* with a particular *nation*.

■ Such nations are not necessarily *nation states*. In the UK, Celtic nationalism has led to the setting up of national parliaments and assemblies for Scotland and Wales respectively. In an extreme form nationalism can lead to *xenophobia* and *racism*.

National Statistics–Socioeconomic Classification (NS–SEC): introduced in 2000, this is an attempt to measure *social class* through the use of a new occupational scale based on the *employment relations* and *market conditions* of workers rather than purely on employment skills.

■ The NS–SEC reflects the massive decline in manufacturing, the huge increase in service industries, especially finance and retail, and the dramatic shift in the proportion of women in the workforce. It recognises eight social classes:

(1) Higher managerial and professional occupations

(2) Lower managerial and professional occupations

(3) Intermediate occupations

(4) Small employers and own account workers

(5) Lower supervisory, craft and related occupations

(6) Semi-routine occupations

(7) Routine occupations

(8) Long-term unemployed and the never-worked

■ This classification no longer divides workers along solely *manual* and *non-manual* lines, e.g. class 3 includes both *blue-* and *white-collar workers*. Categorisation is also by occupation rather than head of household, so women are recognised as workers in their own right.

■ *TIP* It is important to be able to evaluate the strengths and weaknesses of this new scale.

nation state: a modern form of *state* that exercises authority and power over a geographical territory through institutions such as central and local government, a legislature, armed services, a police force and a judiciary.

■ Some nation states contain more than one *nation*, whilst some nations might be split between many nation states.

■ *e.g.* The Kurdish nation is split between the nation states of Turkey and Iraq.

natural sciences: a term for the so-called 'hard sciences' of physics, chemistry and biology that have produced a *positivist* model of scientific enquiry called the *hypothetico-deductive approach*.

■ This approach stresses objectivity, reliability and quantifiability. It has been adopted wholeheartedly by those who believe sociology should be scientific. The logic of the natural sciences has been challenged by philosophers such as Popper, whilst *interpretivist* sociology is sceptical about the emphasis on science as part of sociological enquiry.

nature versus nurture debate: a debate between those who believe human beings inherit characteristics such as intelligence and those who believe such characteristics are the product of social environment and specifically *socialisation*.

■ *Sociobiologists* argue that masculine and feminine characteristics and behaviour are the product of irreversible genetic programmes, i.e. men and women allegedly have a natural predisposition to act in masculine and feminine ways. *Feminists*, on the other hand, see *gender role socialisation* as responsible for femininity and masculinity. They argue that cultural variation in feminine and masculine behaviour undermines biological arguments that genetic differences between male and female are universal.

■ *TIP* The same sort of argument can be applied to intelligence as a possible explanation for educational *underachievement*.

neocolonialism: a Marxist term describing the modern forms that Western exploitation of developing countries now take, such as domination of the terms of international trade, the activities of *multinational* and *transnational companies*, and the *debt dependency* that results from official *aid* programmes.

■ Neocolonialism, according to Marxists, is responsible for the *underdevelopment* of the economy of *less developed countries* along with historical forms of exploitation such as slavery and *colonialism*.

neo-Fordism: the Marxist argument that society is experiencing a new phase of capitalism as *deskilling* and managerial controls increase and more is demanded of workers in terms of quality, range of tasks and time at work.

neo-Marxism: a term used to describe Marxist thinkers who have developed and updated Marx's general theory in the second half of the twentieth century.

new age movement: a collective term used to describe a religion or quasi-religion that focuses on alternative issues such as alternative medicine, environmental philosophies, spiritual fulfilment and paganism and which aims to realise the spiritual potential of its members, sometimes through commercial activities, e.g. new age shops.

■ Davie argues that new age religions affirm the continuing importance of religion in modern societies, albeit in different forms. New age religions may appeal more to women because of their emphasis on healing, cooperation, caring and spirituality.

new criminology: a set of ideas associated with a group of Marxist sociologists, Taylor, Walton and Young, who suggested that working-class people choose to commit crime because of their experience of the injustices of capitalism.

■ They suggest working class-crime is political — it is a conscious reaction of working-class people who see their position at the bottom of the socio-economic hierarchy as being unfair and exploitative. Working-class crime is therefore an attempt to alter capitalism.

■ *e.g.* Crimes against property such as theft and burglary are aimed at the redistribution of wealth whilst vandalism is a symbolic attack on *capitalism's* obsession with property.

■ *TIP* Contrast with *left realism* — this theory is critical of the new criminology and refers to it as over-romanticised left idealism.

n

new evangelical movement: a collective term referring to the proliferation of 'born again' Christians as reflected in the growth of the Pentecostal and Baptist denominations and charismatic house churches.

■ Whereas the established Christian church is experiencing *secularisation,* this sector of Christianity is experiencing an increase in attendance and is especially attractive to young people.

new laddism: the expression of 'lad culture' that became highly visible in the 1990s with the launch of magazines aimed at young men, encouraging them to celebrate sexism, sport, especially football, drinking and pursuing politically incorrect behaviour.

■ Some sociologists suggest that this is a backlash against feminism and the politically correct culture of the 1970s and 1980s.

new left realism: see *left realism.*

newly industrialising country (NIC): sometimes referred to as a Pacific Rim country or an *Asian tiger*, a country which 30 years ago was relatively under-developed but that has since experienced rapid and extensive industrial expansion.

■ *e.g.* Malaysia, Taiwan, South Korea etc.

new man: a media term used to describe an allegedly new type of *masculinity* that emerged in the 1980s, which emphasised sensitivity, caring and being in touch with feelings.

■ It is generally agreed by sociologists that the new man was the product of media hype and that there is little evidence for his existence.

new rabble: a negative term used by the *New Right*, especially Charles Murray, to describe the *underclass.*

new religious movement (NRM): a collective name for *cults* or *sects* used by sociologists such as Wallis.

■ Wallis suggested that NRMs are made up of three types of religious movement: *world-affirming sects* (e.g. scientology), *world-accommodating sects* (e.g. evangelical Christians) and world-rejecting sects (e.g. Moonies). He argues that NRMs originated in the USA, in the middle-class young's sense of *alienation* from the materialism of their parents' culture, the dehumanising experience of work in modern society and disillusion with the US political system because of Vietnam and racism. Later sociological work on religion has added cults to the category of NRMs.

■ *TIP* Be able to illustrate briefly the types of NRM, with examples rationalising their categorisation.

New Right: a group of right-wing Conservative thinkers who stress the need for more individual freedom and responsibility and consequently less state interference in economic and social affairs, especially in the field of welfare.

■ The New Right argue that the *welfare state* had created a dependency culture amongst the unemployed, creating an idle and criminal *underclass*. They believe that the nuclear family is under attack from the easy availability of divorce, homosexuality etc. New Right thinking has made a great contribution to educational reform and the re-organisation of the NHS and social security.

new social movement (NSM): a collective term which refers to a political movement that is broad, middle-class based, and organised around *identity politics* (e.g. the promotion of gay rights, human rights, feminism etc.) or the quality of life of the community (e.g. the protection of the environment etc.).

■ These organisations are less hierarchical and more loose-knit in structure than traditional pressure groups and political parties. Some sociologists see them as a form of *counter-culture* that aims to resist the materialism, *bureaucracy, globalisation* and *alienation* associated with the capitalist world.

news value: an assumption held by editors and journalists about what makes a story newsworthy, i.e. interesting enough to grab a significant audience.

■ Sociologists argue that news-gathering is a selective process, i.e. journalists have to make choices about what to cover and how to cover it.

■ *e.g.* Galtung and Ruge suggest that a story is more likely to be covered if it conforms to the following news values: the unexpectedness of the event, whether it can be reduced to personalities, whether it is simple and clear, whether it is negative because 'bad news is good news' for journalists etc.

■ *TIP* Be aware that Marxists suggest news values are *ideological,* i.e. a story is only selected if it supports the status quo or is critical of views that do not.

new vocationalism: a collection of vocational initiatives (e.g. the Technical, Vocational, Educational Initiative) in the 1980s, targeted at the young unemployed and those still at school, which aimed to equip the young with the skills and education required by a rapidly changing economy.

■ These training and work experience schemes were the direct result of the *New Right* critique that the British workforce in the late 1970s lacked the technical skills required by British industry. However, Marxist sociologists argue that these vocational courses aimed to train young people into taking for granted a future of unskilled, low-paid and alienating work, whilst middle-class students received an academic education in schools, colleges and universities.

new working class: a socioeconomic grouping, allegedly made up of skilled manual workers found in the high-tech computer and electronic industries of the southeast who owned their own homes, did not belong to a trade union and voted Conservative for *instrumental* reasons.

■ In the 1980s Ivor Crewe suggested that this group constituted most of the working-class *deviant vote*, which had ensured Conservative election victories in 1979, 1983 and 1987. However, research has failed to find convincing evidence that such a group exists outside the mainstream working class, although the media are still fond of referring to this group as either 'Essex Man' or 'Mondeo man'.

NIC: see *newly industrialising country.*

non-manual work: traditionally also known as *white-collar work* or mental labour, this type of work is typical of middle-class occupations, officially classified as classes 1 and 2 by the *NS–SEC.*

■ Under the old *Registrar-General's classification of occupations*, social class III NM was composed of clerical workers and was exclusively non-manual. The decline in pay and status of clerks relative to working-class occupations is reflected in their inclusion in the NS–SEC's social class 3, which is made up of manual and non-manual jobs.

non-official statistics: statistics collected by a variety of non-government organisations such as pressure groups, churches, businesses etc.

■ As with *official statistics*, this type of data has to be used with caution.

■ *e.g.* Church attendance and membership statistics are collected by churches and denominations themselves. Some sociologists argue that these provide an insight into the degree of religious belief and *secularisation* in society. However, such statistics may not be the product of reliable and standardised counting procedures. Moreover, as Davie argues, their *validity* is questioned by the fact that many people have religious belief without belonging to a church or belong to a church without having religious belief.

non-response: the failure of potential respondents to return questionnaires or respond to requests for interviews.

■ This problem can create serious problems of *validity*, especially for surveys that rely on postal questionnaires.

■ *e.g.* The Hite Report on sexual behaviour sent out 100,000 questionnaires yet only had a response rate of 3%.

non-work: activities that are not an aspect of paid employment or *domestic labour*, including time spent unemployed, doing leisure activities and on servicing activities, e.g. eating, going to the toilet, sleeping etc.

normlessness: see *anomie*.

norms: the expected cultural rules of social behaviour, which are relative to particular social situations, historical periods, societies and *subcultures* and are enforced by the use of positive and negative *sanctions*.

■ Norms are essentially *values* put into practice. There are norms governing all aspects of human behaviour.

NSM: see *new social movement*.

NS–SEC: see *National Statistics–Socioeconomic Classification*.

nuclear family: a family group consisting of two generations (i.e. parents and children) living in the same household.

■ The *New Right* and *functionalists* subscribe to a *familistic ideology* which suggests that a nuclear ideal should be attained based on marriage, heterosexuality and a traditional *division of labour*. They see the nuclear family as under attack from 'immoral' practices such as cohabitation, divorce and women going out to work. However, evidence suggests that despite *family diversity*, most people are brought up within nuclear households.

■ *TIP* Always challenge the idea that the nuclear family is in decline.

objectivity: a concept applied to the state of mind of the sociologist when designing a research proposal or when analysing evidence, meaning free from *bias*, detached and neutral.

■ *Positivists* believe that scientific research should be objective or *value free*, meaning that the investigation should be free from personal and political opinion and prejudice. Moreover, by adopting certain procedures, e.g. *random sampling* etc., bias should be reduced or eliminated. Finally, they believe that collection of data should not be selective and that findings and methods should be critically evaluated and validated by other sociologists.

observation: an *ethnographic* method, favoured by *interpretivist* sociologists, in which subjects are researched in their natural habitat in an attempt to 'get inside' their heads and understand social life from their point of view.

■ Observation takes a number of forms. Harvey notes it can be informal and take the form of 'hanging about being inquisitive' or it can be the product of casual everyday interaction. Psychologists tend to use observation as a form of surveillance, observing individuals and groups through one-way mirrors. Sociological studies of classroom interaction also tend to take this surveillance form. However, the most popular and common observation method employed by sociologists is *participant observation*.

observer effect: a problem of *validity* associated with *observation* which refers to how the presence of an observer may affect the behaviour of those being observed.

■ This is a form of the *Hawthorne effect*. Some sociologists argue that the use of *covert participant observation* overcomes this problem.

occupational scales: see *Registrar-General's classification of occupations* and *National Statistics–Socioeconomic Classification*.

occupational structure: see *division of labour*.

official aid: see *aid*.

official document: see *document*.

official statistics: statistics collected by local and central government in order to devise *social policies* to assess their success and to plan for future needs.

■ These include registration data relating to births, marriages and deaths.

Governments also produce statistics relating to divorce, crime, morbidity, mortality, poverty, unemployment etc. as well as *census* data every 10 years on the lifestyles of households in the UK. Sociologists use official statistics because they are cheap, readily available and based on large samples. However, statistics must be used with caution because they are *social constructions*, not *social facts*.

■ *e.g.* The most famous use of official statistics by a sociologist was Durkheim's study of *suicide*.

■ *TIP* The problems of crime statistics are a useful way to illustrate the potential problems of official statistics. (See *British Crime Survey, corporate crime, dark figure of crime, radical criminology, self-reports, street crime.*)

old-boy network: the informal network of contacts, supports and services provided in adulthood by ex-public schoolboys for each other, especially those who attended their old school.

■ Sometimes known as the 'old school tie' network, this *mutual support system* provides access to well-paid jobs, especially in the financial sector, for ex-public schoolboys who may not be particularly well qualified. The existence of such a network undermines the notion that the occupational structure is *meritocratic*.

old working class: see *proletarian traditionalist*.

one-parent family: a single- or lone-parent family as a result of the parents' divorce or separation, the death of one parent, or because there has only ever been one parent.

■ The number of one-parent families has increased dramatically over the last 20 years, and they now constitute approximately 20% of all families. Over 90% are headed by females. Most have come about because of divorce or separation. Only 5% of lone parents are teenagers, despite *moral panics* that suggest they are a serious problem. The *New Right* is very critical of one-parent families and argues that they are a root cause of criminality because such families lack an authoritative father figure. *Critical sociologists* argue that such families have been scapegoated and negatively labelled for social problems caused by factors such as recession, which are beyond their control.

■ *TIP* The negative attention paid to one-parent families is probably the result of the emphasis put on nuclear families by *familistic ideology*.

1.2.4 rule of relative hope: the *Oxford mobility study* concluded from analysis of its data that for every working-class male who was upwardly mobile into the service class, two males from the intermediate class achieved the same goal whilst four sons of the service class returned to the class of their fathers.

open/open-ended question: a type of question found in *questionnaires* or used in interviews that leaves the respondent free to answer as he or she chooses, e.g. 'what do you think of the present government?'

open enrolment: the obligation for schools to enrol all applicants until the schools reach full capacity.

■ This was a product of the *Education Reform Act (1988)* and was aimed, along with league tables, at increasing choice for parents as consumers of education.

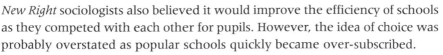

New Right sociologists also believed it would improve the efficiency of schools as they competed with each other for pupils. However, the idea of choice was probably overstated as popular schools quickly became over-subscribed.

open society: a society in which people can move up and down the occupational structure and therefore the class system freely.

■ Western societies are open because they are supposedly *meritocratic*. People are generally recruited to jobs on the basis of *universalistic* educational qualifications. This is in contrast with *closed societies*, which have a system of *ascription* and so there is little or no movement between jobs or social classes.

■ *TIP* Note that the view that Britain is a meritocracy should not be accepted uncritically.

operationalisation: the process of breaking down a *hypothesis* or research aim into measurable and observable components or questions.

■ *Social class* is operationalised by the *NS–SEC* by asking questions relating to *employment relations* and *market conditions*.

opinion leader: according to the *two-step flow model* of media, this is an active individual who has greater exposure to the media than the rest of the audience and who influences others, e.g. friends, relatives etc., with regard to interpretation and effect of media content.

■ This theory suggests that the media's influence on the audience is not as direct as the *hypodermic syringe approach* suggests.

■ *e.g.* Katz and Lazarfeld's research demonstrated that in the fields of consumerism, fashion, films, current affairs and politics, opinion leaders interpreted media messages on behalf of social groups to which they belonged and influenced people to take or not to take certain courses of action, e.g. they saw a poor review of a film and advised their friends not to see it.

opium of the people: a term used by Marx to describe the ideological effects of religion on the working class.

■ Marx argued that religion acted like a drug to dull the pain of oppression. This distracted the working class from the real cause of their problems, i.e. the organisation of capitalism, resulting in *false consciousness*. People sought solace in God and the possibility of an after-life rather than addressing the problem of *exploitation* here and now.

opportunity sampling: see *snowball sampling*.

oppositional leisure: a term used by Parker to describe *leisure* activities that compensate workers for the hazards and physical demands of dangerous jobs, e.g. heavy drinking by North Sea oil workers.

oral history: a type of *life history* technique that records the experiences of ordinary people.

■ Such histories are often combined with letters and diaries to show how ordinary people lived in the past. They give sociologists an alternative picture to that offered by official history and documents that focus almost exclusively on the activities of powerful higher-status groups.

organic solidarity: a concept invented by Durkheim to describe modern industrial societies dominated by interdependence of skills and individualistic values.

■ Durkheim argued that societies characterised by organic solidarity were more likely to experience *anomie* (normlessness), which undermined *community* and led to more destructive and aimless behaviour in modern societies.

organisation: a large grouping of people that exists over time, organised along impersonal lines, usually with a hierarchical *bureaucracy*, with the intention of achieving specific *goals*.

■ Sociologists focus on formal organisations in which activity is planned and regulated in order to achieve particular formal goals, e.g. a school plans educational activity through a curriculum in order that pupils pass exams and gain qualifications. Informal organisations are those created and usually controlled by people working within formal organisations, e.g. business leaders consulting one another at their clubs.

organismic deprivation: a concept used by Glock and Stark to explain why some members of society join religious *sects*.

■ It may be experienced by those who suffer physical and mental health problems.

■ *e.g.* People may turn to sects in the hope of being healed or as an alternative to drugs or alcohol.

outsourcing: subcontracting work that was once carried out within an organisation to external contractors such as consultants.

■ It is often cheaper (especially in terms of a wage-bill, pension contributions etc.) for companies to contract work out on short-term contracts.

over-determinism: a critical concept which suggests that *positivism* exaggerates the power of social factors in shaping human behaviour and neglects people's choices and actions in resisting these social influences.

overt participant observation: see *participant observation*.

ownership and control debate: a media debate focusing on who controls the content of the media and thus how information transmitted to audiences is structured.

■ *Pluralists* argue that ownership of mass media is largely unimportant because audiences drive media output, i.e. if they don't buy or watch the product, media organisations fail. *Instrumental Marxists* argue that the concentration of media ownership in *conglomerates* has led to owners ideologically shaping media content in the interests of the capitalist class. *Structuralist Marxists* agree that media content reflects the capitalist status quo but suggest that this is an accidental by-product of the need to make profit.

■ *TIP* Think about how these three arguments would account for news production.

Oxbridge: a term used to denote Oxford and Cambridge, the two most selective and prestigious universities in the UK.

- Both universities still take the majority of their students from RG social classes I and II and the public schools. Marxists see this as evidence which contradicts the *meritocratic* ideal.

Oxford mobility study: a major study of *social mobility* conducted in 1972 on a survey population of 10,000 men, which found a high *absolute rate of mobility* but concluded from looking at the *relative rate of mobility* that the sons of professional and managerial workers were more likely than the sons of manual workers to obtain top jobs.

- With regard to absolute mobility, the study noted that the children of the working class had moved into service sector jobs in large numbers in the 1950s and 1960s, but this was due to a postwar expansion in the *welfare state* and financial sector rather than a product of *meritocracy*. With regard to relative mobility, the study identified the *1.2.4 rule of relative hope*, which suggests that the service class is able to provide its sons with more advantages than other classes are able to provide for their children.

- **TIP** See *cultural capital* and *intelligence* for alternative explanations for limited working-class upward mobility.

paradigm: a concept, associated with Kuhn, that refers to a powerful set of assumptions and research practices shared by scientists in scientific communities, which other scientists are socialised into and which dominate thinking over a period of time about how science ought to be done.

■ Kuhn notes that paradigms are not the product of an objective search for truth but rather the product of fashion, trends and the distribution of power. Paradigms are eventually overthrown when evidence or anomalies appear that challenge them, although the power of the paradigm may be such that it may take decades for an alternative paradigm to be accepted.

■ *TIP* Kuhn has made an important contribution to the debate about whether sociology should have scientific status.

parity of esteem: a concept used by supporters of the *tripartite system* of education in 1944 which suggested that *secondary modern schools* would enjoy similar status to *grammar schools*.

■ No such thing occurred, as grammar schools attracted more resources, better-qualified staff and greater prestige from parents and employers.

participant observation: an *interpretivist* research method that involves the researcher becoming part of a community in order to study it on an everyday basis in its natural environment.

■ There are a number of different types of participant observation. *Covert participant observation* involves the researcher not revealing his or her identity and pretending to be an ordinary member of the group. The most popular type is the 'observer as participant' in which the researcher tells the group that he or she is conducting research and plays an active role in most group activities. The strength of participant observation is that it produces *qualitative data* rich in *validity*, because it examines people in their natural environment. *Positivists*, however, question its *representativeness* and the *reliability* of such studies, whilst concerns about the *observer effect* and *going native* raise some doubts about the validity of findings.

particularism: a set of internal *values* and *norms* specific to small-scale social groups such as families, tribes etc. that judges people purely on the basis of their *affective* relationships with other people in the group and their *ascribed status*.

■ It is contrasted, especially by *functionalist* sociologists, with the *universalistic* value system used in wider society, which judges people on the basis of what they have or have not achieved.

partisan alignment: the relationship between social class and loyalty to the political party that is supposed to reflect the interests of that class. The idea is also known as class cleavage.

■ In the 1960s, 65% of the working-class vote went to the Labour Party whilst approximately 75–80% of the middle-class vote went to the Conservative Party.

partisan de-alignment: a concept, associated with Ivor Crewe, which suggested that the *new working class* did not automatically identify with the Labour Party throughout the 1980s.

■ Crewe concluded that the Labour vote in the 1980s remained largely working-class but that the working class was no longer largely Labour because the new working class voted on the basis of *instrumental* material interests rather than out of class loyalty.

pathological: term often used in the sociology of crime and deviance to suggest that criminal behaviour is the natural *dysfunctional* outcome of deviant or abnormal *subcultures*.

■ Some sociologists, notably Miller, saw crime and deviance as a natural product of working-class norms and values. Durkheim rejected the view that deviance was pathological and instead argued that it was normal, healthy and *functional* for societies.

patriarchal ideology: a dominant and powerful set of ideas that aim to reproduce, maintain and legitimate gender inequalities, i.e. male dominance and female subordination, in areas of social life such as jobs, education, family life, media etc.

■ Feminists believe that both males' and females' first contact with patriarchal ideology is through *gender role socialisation*.

■ *e.g.* The basic sentiments of patriarchal ideology suggest that femininity involves particular passive qualities, that women's main goals ought to be attained through romantic love, children and looking after a family and that they are better suited to a subordinate supporting role compared with men. Feminist research has identified such thinking underpinning *familistic ideology*, *media representations* of females, and state *social policy*.

patriarchy: broadly defined as male dominance over women.

■ Walby suggests that it can be broken down into three components: first, *subordination*, i.e. in most social institutions women are defined as less important than men; second, *oppression*, i.e. women are actively discriminated against; and third, *exploitation*, i.e. men take for granted women's skills and labour without rewarding them. Feminists therefore use the concept of patriarchy to describe the unequal distribution of power between women and men, although the various feminist theoretical positions, i.e. *liberal feminism, black feminism, Marxist feminism, radical feminism* and *triple systems theory*, differ in their analysis and proposed solutions.

p

■ *TIP* Patriarchy is a key concept and just as important as social class and ethnicity in explaining inequality in modern Britain.

patrilineal: descent or inheritance of titles, property, surname etc. through the male line.

peer group: a friendship group made up of individuals who are of a similar age and status and who may subscribe to similar values and norms, especially in relation to leisure.

■ The peer group is thought to be an important agency of *secondary socialisation* in adolescence. Some peer groups may develop a fairly rigid set of values and norms that may differ from those held by mainstream society, i.e. they may evolve into deviant *subcultures.*

personal document: sometimes called a document of life, it includes diaries, letters, biographies, photographs, suicide notes and even inscriptions on gravestones, all of which give sociologists insight into how people subjectively see the social world.

■ The use of personal documents is an *unobtrusive method* that produces *qualitative data.* It is suitable for research that requires in-depth detail, such as a *case study* of an individual or social group to which the individual belongs. However, *positivist* sociologists question the *representativeness* of such sources, i.e. are people who leave personal documents typical of the population at large? There may also be a problem of *reliability*, e.g. significant time may have lapsed between an event and the recording of it. Finally, the *validity* of the data may be questioned, e.g. it may only reflect one particular point of view.

perspective: a broad set of ideas or theories that aims to explore how the social world is organised, e.g. *functionalism, Marxism, feminism, positivism* and *interpretivism.*

petty bourgeoisie: a Marxist term meaning the self-employed, or those who employ very few labourers.

■ Between 1981 and 1991 the number of self-employed rose from 6.7% of the workforce to over 10%. The character of the self-employed up to the 1980s mainly reflected its retail and personal services dominance. However, the number of self-employed engaged in business consultancies and information technology rose in the 1980s and 1990s due to *outsourcing.* There is also some evidence that the petty bourgeoisie may be adopting more militant practices in defence of their interests, e.g. the petrol protests in 2000.

phenomenology: see *interpretive sociology.*

pilot survey or interview: a 'dress rehearsal' in which a *questionnaire* is given to a few individuals, or a couple of *interviews* are conducted, in order to uncover potential research problems relating to *response rates*, questionnaire design, suitability of *sample* and efficiency of interviewers.

pluralism: a sociological theory which argues that power is widely distributed in society amongst a plurality of competing *pressure groups.*

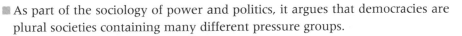

■ As part of the sociology of power and politics, it argues that democracies are plural societies containing many different pressure groups.

■ *e.g.* The role of the state is to mediate between competing demands for power and influence. As part of the sociology of the media, pluralism argues that audiences rather than owners, editors or journalists shape media content.

polarisation: a Marxist concept that describes the process of the capitalist class getting richer and the proletariat getting poorer, which Marx predicted would lead to the working class eventually realising and acting upon their exploited and subordinate position and becoming a *class-for-itself*.

■ However, the experience of polarisation has been tempered by dramatic improvements in the material circumstances of the working class, which modern Marxists argue have resulted in them experiencing *false consciousness*.

policing: sociological interest in policing has focused on how policing strategies and the actions of individual police officers contribute to the social construction of *official statistics* on crime.

■ *Critical sociologists* suggest that the over-proportionate number of working-class and black people in the criminal statistics may be the result of the police paying more attention to these groups rather than the groups being prone to more criminality.

political socialisation: the process by which people acquire and internalise a political awareness or consciousness, usually from parents, peer group and community, but also from the acquisition of education, the experience of work, and exposure to *media representations*.

polyandry: an extremely rare type of marriage system in which a woman is allowed to have more than one husband.

■ *e.g.* In remote areas of Nepal and Tibet, several brothers may be married to one wife.

polygamy: a type of marriage system in which a person can have more than one spouse at any one time.

■ In societies in which such arrangements are legal, the most common type is *polygyny*. Polygamy tends to be illegal in the West, where only *monogamy* is allowed.

polygyny: a type of marriage system in which a man can have more than one wife at any one time.

polysemic: a term describing media texts which refers to the possibility that they may be 'read' or interpreted in more than one way by different audiences.

■ It is associated with *semiology*.

popular culture: the culture of ordinary people, which is seen to be dominated by mass-produced forms of entertainment (i.e. *mass culture*) such as Hollywood films, television, pop music etc.

■ Critics of popular culture suggest that it is 'low culture' and considerably less valuable than *high culture*. Others argue that working-class culture is in decline

p

because popular culture is dominated by American *cultural imperialism*. Marxists are concerned that popular culture is the new *opium of the people* that aims to reinforce the *false consciousness* of the working class.

population: sociologists have focused on the high population growth of *less developed countries* and its impact upon *development*.

▪ Some sociologists believe that the developing world is experiencing a population explosion and this is putting too much strain on the limited resources and *infrastructure* of these societies, thus causing poverty. Such sociologists advocate family-planning policies (as in China) and health education for women as solutions. However, Marxists argue that the real problem is not population but inequalities in the distribution of land and wealth. Poverty leads to high population because children are economic assets. Moreover, Western consumption of food and energy far exceeds that of the developing world.

positive discrimination: social policies which aim to establish material equality for social groups such as women and ethnic minorities.

▪ Such groups may be denied access to education and jobs by the majority group in a society because of deeply entrenched institutional bias.

▪ *e.g.* Social policies such as *affirmative action* in the USA aimed to force institutions to recruit a certain number of women and members of ethnic minority groups in the 1970s. In the UK, *compensatory education* programmes in the 1960s aimed to increase funding for primary schools in deprived parts of Britain named as *educational priority areas*.

positivism: an approach to society and the methods required to study its organisation that assumes society exists independently of individuals (i.e. we are born into society and we die, but society continues to exist) and that human behaviour is shaped by social laws over which we have little control.

▪ Positivism is the search for laws of social behaviour using the logic and methods of the *natural sciences*. It favours certain methods, e.g. the *social survey*, and emphasises the scientific characteristics of *reliability, objectivity* and quantifiable data. Its main critic is *interpretive sociology*.

postal questionnaires: questionnaires sent through the post to respondents.

▪ These share the strengths and weaknesses of conventional questionnaires but with the added problem of the potential of greater *non-response*.

postfeminism: the *postmodern* assumption that feminism is merely another *metanarrative* that is largely ineffective in explaining the condition of women because womanhood in postmodern society is characterised by a plurality of female identities.

post-Fordism: the argument that mass production techniques such as assembly-line production are giving way to more flexible computer-based methods of production, based on meeting demand for specialised or exclusive products for particular groups or lifestyles.

▪ Critics of post-Fordism argue that the decline of mass production is greatly exaggerated. It has merely been relocated to low-cost developing countries.

p

postindustrial society: the idea, mainly associated with Daniel Bell, that modern societies are more geared to the production of knowledge, information and services than manufacturing.

▨ This has led to a transformation in work practices, as the *tertiary sector*, which is involved in the processing of knowledge and information, increases dramatically. Critics such as *neo-Fordists* suggest that *capitalism* has entered a new stage of development in that the tertiary sector is simply more profitable for investment and exploitation than manufacturing.

postmodern/postmodernity: the economic and social characteristics associated with the postmodern world.

▨ It is argued that manufacturing is in decline in the postmodern world. Postmodern economic life revolves around branding and the processing of information. *Transnational* companies through an international *division of labour* control what manufacturing of goods still exists. Moreover, postmodern societies are thought to be 'media-saturated'. This has resulted in the world becoming a global village in which people from a diverse and broad range of backgrounds share consumption of global information and entertainment. The dominance of media transnationals has led to some concerns that postmodern culture emphasises style at the expense of content. However, postmodernists argue that postmodern culture is rich and substantial because it emphasises the relativity of knowledge, ideas and lifestyle which means that choice and diversity are celebrated.

poverty: see *absolute poverty* and *relative poverty*.

poverty cycle: see *cycle of deprivation*.

poverty line: an income level estimated to be the absolute minimum needed for subsistence in terms of food, rent and clothing.

▨ The *absolute poverty* studies of Booth and Rowntree used poverty lines.

▨ *e.g.* Rowntree established an absolute poverty line based on nutritional needs, clothes and shelter. Governments use poverty lines too in that people become eligible for benefits if their income falls below a set level.

poverty trap: People who earn under a certain income (a *poverty line*) qualify for *means-tested* benefits, but if their income rises a few pounds above that line, they lose out financially because either they lose the benefit or it is reduced.

▨ A variation relates to those slightly above the official poverty line who do not qualify for benefits but who, after tax and national insurance, are worse off than those on benefits; they may be better off giving up work and claiming benefits.

power: defined by Weber as being able to impose one's will on another despite resistance.

▨ Weber identifies two main types of power, i.e. *coercion* or violent force and *legitimate authority*, which is underpinned by consent. There exists a sociological debate about the distribution of power in modern societies.

■ **e.g.** *Pluralists* claim power is widely diffused and distributed among a variety of community *elites*, whilst elite theory and Marxism claim power is concentrated in the hands of elites and a *capitalist* class respectively.

power elite: a concept used by C. Wright Mills to describe a single ruling minority made up of inter-connected groups — the business, political and military elites — who run the USA in their own interest.

■ **TIP** See John Scott's concept of the *establishment* in order to further your understanding of power elites in the UK.

powerlessness: a concept used by *left realism* to account for street crime among young working-class and ethnic minority youth.

■ Young and Lea note that such youth experience *relative deprivation* compared with their *peer group* who have jobs and a steady income. Moreover, they are marginalised in that they have no *pressure groups* working on their behalf. Politicians show little interest in them, whilst the police pay them undue attention. The feelings of powerlessness generated by these processes may lead to confrontation with the police, riots or crime.

preindustrial society: according to Durkheim and Tönnies, this is characterised by strong *social order, community, ascription, particularism* and *collective conscience*.

■ Durkheim sees preindustrial society as characterised by *mechanical solidarity* whilst Tönnies associates it with *Gemeinschaft*. Parsons sees multifunctional *extended families* as typical of this period, although in contrast the historian Peter Laslett's research indicates that nuclear families may have been the norm because of early death, late marriage and the practice of sending some children away to become servants and apprentices.

prejudice: generally a stereotypical or negative view of an individual or social group that is not supported by the facts.

■ Prejudice is usually aimed at powerless minority groups, e.g. ethnic minorities, homosexuals, the disabled, females etc.

pressure group: a political interest group that exists in order to persuade governments to reform existing policy or to introduce new policy.

■ There are two types of pressure group. Interest or *sectional groups* aim to protect the interests of their members, e.g. trade unions. *Promotional groups* focus on specific issues and causes, e.g. Age Concern.

■ **TIP** Political sociology has recently moved away from the study of pressure groups to the examination of *new social movements*.

prestige: the *status* attached to an individual or group because of their social or occupational position.

primary data: data collected first-hand by sociologists using *questionnaires, interviews, observation* etc.

primary deviance: a concept used by Lemert to describe deviant acts before they are publicly labelled.

■ Lemert suggests that an understanding of *secondary deviance* is more important than primary deviance because the latter has few consequences for a person's identity and status compared with the former.

primary labour market: that sector of employment in which jobs are secure and well paid, with promotion opportunities, fringe benefits etc.

▧ The primary labour market is focused on by the *dual labour market* theory, which points out that it is dominated by white males in contrast with the *secondary labour market*, which is dominated by female and ethnic minority workers.

primary research: research carried out by sociologists which results in the collection of *primary data.*

▧ *TIP* Contrast with *secondary research* and *secondary data.*

primary sector: that part of the economy that is concerned with the extraction of raw materials (e.g. coal, fishing, agriculture) or their processing (e.g. iron and steel, shipbuilding etc.)

primary socialisation: the initial socialisation into culture that takes place throughout childhood within the family group.

▧ *Functionalists* like Parsons see the function of primary socialisation as structuring the personality of children, especially in regard to equipping them with key values such as the motivation to achieve.

▧ *e.g.* Two central aspects of the socialisation process within families are the development of a conscience, which to some extent is structured by use of positive and negative *sanctions* (i.e. rewards and punishment) and the development of imitation, in that children view their parents as *role models* and may copy their behaviour. This may be a central influence in *gender role socialisation.*

private medicine: health care services that are only available to those who can pay for them through private health insurance.

▧ In the 1980s private health was encouraged by the Conservative government as part of its policy of reducing state involvement in providing public services, encouraging individual responsibility and increasing choice for consumers.

private school: a school outside the state sector, requiring the payment of fees.

▧ Private schools take a variety of forms. The most prestigious are called public schools, e.g. Eton, Harrow, Charterhouse etc., and provide the most glittering prizes of all — direct routes to Oxford and Cambridge universities (*Oxbridge*) — although this is largely because of the historical relationship they enjoy with these institutions rather than because of the superior ability of their pupils. Below the public schools are approximately 3,000 private preparatory and secondary schools. Some of these specialise in religion, music, dance etc. Marxists argue that as long as private education continues to exist, *meritocracy* is impossible, because evidence suggests that those who were educated privately are disproportionately found in top jobs, mainly because of *social closure* and the *old-boy network*. The *New Right* suggests that the existence of such schools is central to the concepts of parental choice and individual responsibility.

private sector: that part of the economy which aims to provide services such as education and health in a competitive market environment.

■ Contrast with the *public sector.*

private sphere: the domestic sphere, which is associated with women and children.

■ It is often contrasted with the *public sphere*, which is associated with men. There is some evidence that young women today are more likely to reject the private sphere than women of previous generations, as illustrated by the increasing numbers of women choosing not to have children and focusing on careers rather than relationships.

privatisation: the selling of state assets such as the railways, gas, electricity, water etc. to private enterprise.

■ The Conservative government of 1979–97 was responsible for selling a great number of assets, which reflected its ideological commitment to reducing state intervention.

privatised instrumental worker: see *instrumental collectivism* and *privatised working class*.

privatised nuclear family: see *privatised working class*.

privatised working class: essentially, *instrumental collectivist* workers who work primarily to provide a good standard of living for their immediate family and spend most of their leisure time with their spouse and children.

■ There is some concern that such privatisation or home-centredness may be the result of *popular culture* — television, in particular — and that the emphasis on consumerism may encourage families to be inward- rather than outward-looking. Privatised families are seen by some to be a symptom of the *loss of community*.

probability sampling: see *random sampling*.

professions: a middle-class occupational group characterised by a high level of technical and intellectual expertise acquired after an intensive and extensive period of training, high financial rewards and status, high standards of conduct and public service, usually regulated by membership of a professional body.

■ Savage notes that professionals are the most secure of occupational groups within the middle class. This group is likely to recruit internally, i.e. sons and daughters of professionals tend to end up as professionals too, because parents are able to pass on both economic and *cultural capital* to their children. Functionalist sociologists see professionals as essentially altruistic, i.e. as serving the public interest. Marxists see them working on behalf of capitalism to maintain the health and productivity of workers, whilst Friedson suggests that *altruism* is merely an occupational strategy that ensures professional control over recruitment, training and working practices and maintains high financial rewards.

proletarianisation: the idea, associated with Harry Braverman, that sections of the middle class, specifically clerical workers, have experienced a decline in their *market conditions* and *status* and consequently lost the social and economic advantages they traditionally enjoyed over the working class.

■ Braverman argues that technology, especially computers, has *deskilled* the complex tasks of *white-collar workers*. Moreover, white-collar work has been feminised as women have been employed at low rates of pay to perform the simple and repetitive routines brought about by deskilling. Braverman therefore claims that white-collar workers have been absorbed into the working class.

proletarian traditionalist: a type of manual worker, likely to be living in a traditional working-class community, who feels a strong sense of working-class identity and a keen sense of worker solidarity and loyalty because of shared work experience.

■ Virtually all aspects of their lives, i.e. attitudes towards family and community, political affiliation and use of leisure, will be a product of a keen sense of working-class identity.

■ *e.g.* Such workers tend to see modern society as characterised by conflict and consequently subscribe to a 'them versus us' mentality. It is thought that such workers are in decline because of recession and unemployment. Some sociologists claim most workers today are *instrumental collectivists*.

proletariat: the Marxist term for the working class, whose *labour power* is exploited by the *bourgeoisie*.

promotional group: a pressure group that promotes specific interests, usually to do with some aspect of identity (e.g. gay rights) or a single issue (e.g. environmentalism).

■ Some sociologists have renamed these groups *new social movements*.

Protestant work ethic: a set of values, originating in the Protestant Calvinist religion, that have generally become part of commonsense beliefs about how economic success might be achieved, i.e. through self-discipline, hard work, thrift and rejection of idleness and self-indulgence.

■ Weber argued that religious ideas like these had initiated the economic and social conditions in which capitalism had emerged at the end of the eighteenth century.

■ *e.g.* The adoption of the Protestant work ethic led to the rapid accumulation of capital and the emergence of a Calvinist capitalist class at the end of the feudal era.

proto-communities: groups of people who do not occupy the same physical or geographical space but nonetheless share a common imagination and lifestyle and demonstrate their common belonging to the group in symbolic ways.

■ Such communities tend to be made up of younger people who are keen to display their shared identity through the consumption of brands and logos, similar styles of dress and taste in music, and the adoption of particular ways of speaking. They are thought to be a typical product of *postmodern* societies.

■ *e.g.* The cyber-communities found in internet chat-rooms are typical proto-communities in that they often come together on-line to consume and celebrate a shared interest, but are unlikely ever to meet physically.

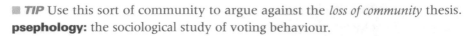

■ *TIP* Use this sort of community to argue against the *loss of community* thesis.

psephology: the sociological study of voting behaviour.

psychic deprivation: a concept used by Glock and Stark to explain why some members of society join religious *sects*.

■ Those who are psychically deprived may be searching for more than what the dominant value system offers. They may wish for some inner spiritual fulfilment rather than the materialist goals on offer in capitalist societies.

■ *e.g.* Sects such as the Divine Light Mission, Transcendental Meditation (TM) and the Moonies claim to offer this. Such cults tend to be attractive to the middle class and the young.

public school: see *private school*.

public sector: services such as education, health, welfare etc. maintained by the *state*.

public sphere: areas of social life dominated by men, including paid employment and leisure spaces such as pubs, clubs and football matches.

■ It can be argued that the evening is a public sphere dominated by men. Women's chances of being attacked increase at night and women found alone in night-time environments may find themselves labelled as sexually available. The public sphere and private sphere division is an aspect of *patriarchy*.

purposive sampling: the choice of a particular group or place to study because it fits the type of group or place the sociologist is interested in studying.

■ *e.g.* The types of sample used by *observation* studies are often purposive.

qualitative data: data collected from *unstructured interviews*, letters, *diaries* and *observation* that are usually presented textually in the form of extracts from conversations, verbatim replies to interview questions or detailed descriptions of social encounters or processes.

■ They are usually richer and more detailed than *quantitative data*. They are naturalistic in that they usually focus on how respondents view the social world. The data speak for themselves. They are consequently favoured by *interpretivists*. *Positivists* are sceptical about the *reliability* of the methods used to collect such data. They are particularly critical of the way that such data are presented because the intentions or motives of the respondents may be misinterpreted by the reader.

quantitative data: statistical data derived from methods such as *questionnaires* and *structured interviews* that can be presented in the form of tables, charts, graphs, diagrams etc.

■ *Positivists* prefer such information because groups of statistics can be compared in order to establish cause and effect relationships and therefore uncover possible social laws. *Interpretivists* are critical because statistics do not give insight into how people interpret the social world they inhabit.

■ *TIP* It is very important when confronted by quantitative information in the form of tables, charts, graphs etc. that the organisation of the data in terms of scale and time-span be examined.

questionnaire: a set of standardised questions that are distributed by hand or post for respondents to fill in.

■ Questionnaires are normally used as part of the *social survey* method and aimed at large *samples*. They are preferred by *positivists* because all respondents are subjected to the same stimuli, mainly in the form of *closed questions*. Consequently, they are regarded as highly reliable. Moreover, they produce large amounts of quantifiable data. *Interpretivists* criticise the *validity* of questionnaire data because questionnaires are an artificial method that attract artificial responses, i.e. the person is reacting to the questionnaire, which may be interpreted as 'intrusive', 'threatening', 'official' etc. The use of closed questions with fixed responses means that the sociologists end up imposing their interpretation of a situation on the respondents. Moreover, the use of closed questions makes it difficult for respondents to convey their feelings, interpretations etc.

quota sampling: a method of *sampling* usually used by market researchers who are interested in stopping and interviewing specific types of people, e.g. housewives.

■ It is generally regarded as a quick and cheap method of picking a sample but it is not regarded as *reliable* or *objective* because it depends upon the researcher's interpretation of who is suitable or who will cooperate and who will not. Criteria for this might differ from researcher to researcher.

race: the classification of human beings into different biological groups on the basis of physical characteristics such as skin colour.

▓ Sociologists are sceptical of the value of this concept because there is no scientific evidence of innate differences of *intelligence* or personality between races.

race relations: the social relations between ethnic or racial groups which have been the subject of attention from sociologists and politicians and which have resulted in legislation aimed at countering *racial prejudice, racial discrimination* and *social inequality.*

racial discrimination: *racial prejudice* put into practice.

▓ *o.g.* By refusing to give people jobs, promotion or housing on the basis of skin colour or other 'racial' characteristics, and by physically and verbally abusing people from ethnic minorities through racially motivated attacks and name-calling.

racial prejudice: a type of negative thinking, usually about ethnic minorities, that is shaped by factually incorrect, exaggerated and distorted stereotypes.

racism: a combination of discriminatory beliefs and behaviour, based on the unfounded assumption that a racial or *ethnic minority* group is inferior, that is used to justify social, economic and political inequalities.

▓ Weberians see such practices and beliefs arising out of status and power differences, whilst Marxists see racism as a capitalist *ideology* that functions to divide and rule the working class, so distracting their attention away from class inequality.

radical criminology: a *Marxist* perspective on crime and deviance which suggests that the *official statistics* on crime are ideological.

▓ Such statistics are allegedly constructed by capitalist agents such as the police in order deliberately to criminalise the working class (and therefore legitimate greater social control) and so distract from crimes committed by the powerful, e.g. *corporate* and *white-collar crime.*

radical feminism: a feminist perspective which argues that *patriarchy* pervades all aspects of culture and social life and that all women are oppressed by men, regardless of cultural, class or ethnic differences.

- At its most basic, radical feminism argues that men are the enemy. The family is seen as the main agency of male oppression of womanhood and consequently radical feminists have been concerned to demonstrate how male power is exercised and legitimated.

- *e.g.* Patriarchy is seen to be present in personal relationships such as marriage, roles such as child-rearing, *housework* and practices such as *domestic violence*, rape and prostitution. Radical feminists argue that 'the personal is political' and some argue that even the act of sexual intercourse between consenting couples is exploitative and benefits men more than women. Moreover, women's culture, knowledge, experience and subjective interpretations are said to be devalued by men. Radical feminists conclude that the only way women can be free of patriarchy is if they live separately from men. Radical feminists have been criticised for defining patriarchy too broadly and failing to consider that there may be variations in the nature of oppression. Moreover, they have been accused of neglecting other sources of exploitation and subordination based on class, ethnicity and age.

- *TIP* Be able to compare this type of feminism with *liberal feminism, black feminism, Marxist feminism, triple systems theory* and *rational choice theory* when considering *gender stratification* and inequality.

radical psychiatry: a form of social psychiatry, popular in the 1960s and 1970s, and particularly associated with R. D. Laing and David Cooper. It suggested that the origins of mental illness might lie in the social and economic organisation of modern societies and especially family relationships.

- Laing and Cooper were very sceptical of the functionalist idea that the family provides emotional support for children. They argued instead that the family 'terrorises' children by destroying their free will, imagination and creativity and consequently it turns children into conformist automatons. Laing goes so far as to suggest that some family members may become schizophrenic as a result of these processes.

random sampling: a method of social research which aims to ensure that the group being studied is a *representative sample* of the wider population by choosing individuals at random.

- The most common types of random sampling method are *systematic* and *stratified sampling*.

rational choice theory: an argument associated with Catherine Hakim, who suggests that feminism has propagated a number of myths about gender inequalities in employment, especially the view that the forces of *patriarchy* are preventing women from competing with men in the workplace.

- Hakim argues that women's career aspirations and commitment to work are not as strong as men's, and lack of free childcare is not the main obstacle in women's employment.

- *e.g.* She argues that the key reason for gender inequality in the workplace is women's rational choice not to take up work opportunities because they choose other options, i.e. they choose to put children and home first. Hakim has been criticised for seeing women making these choices in a cultural vacuum, i.e. she neglects the cultural pressures on women to have children or to feel guilt if they don't stay at home and look after their children. Feminists argue that women's 'choices' are shaped by such cultural pressures.

rationalisation: a concept used by Weber to describe the process whereby behaviour and beliefs based on emotion or tradition, e.g. religious beliefs, which characterised *preindustrial societies*, have been replaced by rational-scientific behaviour and beliefs which revolve around organisation, regulation and precise measurement.

■ Weber saw rationalisation as a defining feature of capitalist society that is reflected in the nation state, which is based upon *rational-legal* authority, and modern organisations, with their bureaucratic hierarchies pursuing rational goals. Sociologists such as Wilson argue that rationalisation is one aspect of secularisation.

rational-legal authority: a type of *power* that is institutionalised, administered by a hierarchical bureaucracy and generally accepted by the majority of society as legitimate because it is seemingly impartially applied to all and enforced without bias.

realism: a theoretical position that attempts to reconcile the differences between *positivism* and *interpretivism*.

■ It is influenced by the *natural sciences* in terms of methods and procedures. Like *positivism*, it views society as an objective reality made up of systems characterised by social processes such as *ideology, power* etc. However, it also takes the *interpretivist* view that people's behaviour can create and transform the social world. Realists aim to combine these two theoretical positions to explore the hidden or underlying causes of social phenomena. Realism has made a significant contribution to the debate about whether sociology is a science and to the subject of crime and deviance via *left realism*.

realist theory of science: a critique of *positivism* which points out that many sciences are engaged in the study of unobservable phenomena rather than hard *empirical* data, e.g. seismology, meteorology and astronomy, and therefore cannot make precise predictions about the behaviour of the phenomena they are studying.

■ Realists refer to such sciences as open sciences. Sociology could be classed as an open science because it is concerned with explaining underlying social processes and structures.

reception analysis: a theory of *media effects* which argues that the audience is composed of media-literate individuals who actively engage in the interpretation of media messages.

■ Using ethnographic methods, researchers such as Morley have found that a range of interpretations of media content exist among audiences, which are partly socially shaped by factors such as class, education, family structure etc.

■ *TIP* Reception analysis is similar to some aspects of *uses and gratifications theory* and like that theory should be used as a critique of the *hypodermic syringe approach*.

reconstituted family: a family that comprises divorced or widowed parents who have remarried and children from the previous marriage or *cohabitation*.

■ The number of such families has increased significantly in the last decade because of divorce, e.g. approximately 1 in 12 children were living in this type of family in the mid-1990s. It is likely that family life in reconstituted families is experienced quite differently from that in a conventional family unit because children probably have close ties with the family of the parent who no longer lives with them. They may find themselves pulled in two different directions and consequently have tense relationships with their step-parents. These families are further complicated if the parents decide to have children of their own.

refutation: see *falsification*.

Registrar-General's classification of occupations: measurement of social class used by the government until 2000, when it was replaced by the *NS–SEC*.

■ It divided the population into five broad social classes, and was based on the idea that employment skills are a good indicator of income, lifestyle, education and status.

I   Professional
II   Managerial and technical
III NM Skilled non-manual
III M Skilled manual
IV   Semi-skilled manual
V   Unskilled manual

reification: the treatment of a social phenomenon such as society as if it is an independent thing existing externally to the individuals who comprise it, and having its own qualities and characteristics.

■ *Positivists* tend to view society in this way. They see society as existing above and beyond the individual in that people are born into a society that already exists and when they die, society continues without them.

relative deprivation (1): feelings of deprivation that derive from individuals or social groups comparing themselves with similar individuals or groups.

■ This concept is central to the *left realist* explanation for street crime. Young and Lea suggest that working-class and black youth feel relatively deprived compared with their middle-class and white peers respectively in terms of jobs, income, access to designer consumer goods etc. Such feelings combined with the frustration associated with feelings of being powerless to change their situation motivate criminal behaviour. However, despite the influence of this theory, there is little empirical evidence to support the view that delinquency is motivated by relative deprivation.

relative deprivation (2): see *relative poverty*.

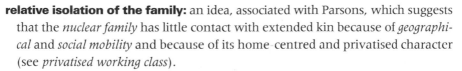

relative isolation of the family: an idea, associated with Parsons, which suggests that the *nuclear family* has little contact with extended kin because of *geographical* and *social mobility* and because of its home-centred and privatised character (see *privatised working class*).

■ Empirical evidence suggests that nuclear families, despite geographical distance, maintain regular contact with extended kin, especially grandparents, and subscribe to the view that family members have obligations to support each other socially, economically and emotionally. The degree of such contact depends on a range of factors including social class, ethnicity, geographical distance etc.

■ *e.g.* *Divorce, remarriage* and the growing numbers of *reconstituted families* increase rather than decrease contact between extended kin. It is generally accepted that nuclear families are active contributors to loose-knit extended *kinship networks*.

■ *TIP* See also *local, dispersed, modified* and *attenuated extended family*.

relative poverty: Townsend defined this type of poverty as lacking the resources to enjoy the living conditions, amenities and rituals that the mass of society takes for granted, e.g. income, housing, education, health etc.

■ This definition assumes that definitions of poverty are not fixed — they reflect constantly changing living standards and changing cultural expectations.

■ *e.g.* Poverty may even differ between different groups within the same society because different regions, age groups etc. may have different social needs, e.g. the elderly may need access to a different set of resources from those required by pregnant women.

■ *TIP* Note that the strengths and weaknesses of this definition of poverty are the weaknesses and strengths of the definition of *absolute poverty*.

relative rate of mobility: the comparison of rates of *intergenerational mobility* between different social classes.

■ The *Oxford mobility study* found that some social groups were more likely than others to fill the top service jobs as encapsulated in their *1.2.4 rule of relative hope*, which showed that the *service class* was able to provide its sons with more advantages than other classes were able to provide for their children.

reliable/reliability: a concept associated with research methods, which are said to be reliable if the research can be repeated exactly by another researcher and provide the same results.

■ The concept therefore focuses on replication of methodology and is one of the foundation stones of *positivist* scientific sociology.

■ *e.g.* Certain methods such as *questionnaires* and *structured interviews* are thought to be high in reliability, whilst methods preferred by *interpretivist* sociologists such as *unstructured interviews* and *participant observation*, which depend on personal relationships being established between the sociologist and the respondents, are often criticised for being unreliable.

religion: a complex concept that can be defined either in terms of its functions, i.e. what it does, or in terms of its substantive content, i.e. its key features, such as belief in God etc.

■ Many sociologists combine the two approaches. Durkheim defined religion as a set of beliefs and practices related to the sacred, i.e. things set apart from ordinary society, and set about analysing its functions for society. Marx mainly focused on the functional, e.g. how religion functioned as an ideological tool of capitalism. Some sociologists have extended the functional definition of religion to include *civil religion* and religious surrogates such as football, because many of the practices associated with these function in a similar way to those associated with religion. Whatever definition is adopted, it has implications for *secularisation* theory, which suggests religion in the UK is in decline.

religiosity: the extent of religious belief and practice, which in the modern UK is said to be in decline as measured by attitude surveys, church attendance and membership.

■ However, whether religiosity is in decline depends upon how we define it. Believers in *secularisation* tend to adopt a very narrow definition of religiosity that focuses on going to church. This is problematical because, as Davie argues, modern religious belief and practice may be characterised by belonging without believing and believing without belonging. Also, if a wider definition of religiosity is adopted, i.e. religion is concerned with the uncertain, it becomes extremely difficult to quantify.

religious pluralism: an aspect of the *secularisation* theory which suggests that the monolithic religions of the past no longer minister to all members of society because they have fragmented into a marketplace of religions competing for 'spiritual shoppers'.

remarriage: the act of entering another marriage after divorce.

■ Remarriages now constitute one third of all marriages, which supports the argument that marriage is not in decline. People are dissatisfied with specific marriages rather than the institution of marriage itself. Moreover, remarriage may indicate that people are demanding higher standards from marriage and their partners today, and are no longer willing to contemplate *empty-shell marriages*.

replication: the act of repeating a piece of research as it was designed, usually by another researcher, in order to verify its findings and so confirm the *reliability* of the original research method.

■ Despite *positivist* emphasis on this major characteristic of scientific method, in practice it rarely occurs because funding is rarely available and/or there is no status in repeating someone else's research.

representativeness: whether individuals making up the *sample* are typical of the wider social group, or the situation being studied is typical of social life in that particular community etc.

■ *Positivist* researchers put emphasis on this quality because the large-scale social survey method they favour usually aims to generalise to the larger group to which the sample belongs. They consequently focus on using *random sampling* methods, which they claim minimise *bias* and ensure the representativeness of the sample. Positivists tend to be critical of what they see as the lack of representativeness in *interpretivist* research because it tends to focus on very small samples or exotic and deviant groups that may not be typical of mainstream society.

representative sample: a sample of the research population which in terms of its characteristics mirrors the larger population so that findings from that sample can be generalised to the wider group.

repressive state apparatus (RSA): a Marxist concept that refers to the forces of *coercion*, e.g. the armed forces, secret police, police, judiciary etc., which the capitalist state has at its disposal when faced by internal or external threats to its security, authority and legitimacy.

■ The Marxist Althusser noted that such agencies were rarely used in capitalist societies because *ideological state apparatuses* (ISAs) ensured *hegemony* and therefore rule by consent.

■ *e.g.* Both RSAs and ISAs function primarily to reproduce, maintain and legitimate class inequality and to manage the potential conflict that might arise out of the exploitative nature of the capitalist order.

resacrilisation: the idea that the growth of *new religious movements* reflects a renewed interest and belief in religion and therefore a religious revival.

■ This argument originates with Greeley and Nelson and is used by them to counter the *desacrilisation* aspect of the *secularisation* debate.

reserve army of labour: a Marxist idea which suggests that women and ethnic minorities are only brought into the labour force in times of economic boom, when demand for labour rises, and are the first groups to be discarded when the economy goes into recession.

■ Moreover, their existence is used by employers as a threat to coerce workers into accepting low rates of pay and/or to undermine industrial action. Women are persuaded to accept this exploited role because they are convinced by *familistic ideology*, which says that they should put domestic roles, especially child-rearing, before career aspirations. *Institutional racism* ensures that there is little protest about the treatment of ethnic minorities, many of whom experience unemployment as a fact of life. However, the extensive movement of women into the labour force in recent years suggests that this theory may be dated.

resistance: a term used by *interpretivist* sociologists who argue that people are conscious choice-making individuals who can resist structural influences and social processes such as negative labelling by *agencies of social control* either on an individual level or as part of a *subcultural* response.

■ This concept is generally used to illustrate the view that some structural theories, in particular functionalism and Marxism, subscribe to an *over-deterministic* view of human behaviour.

■ *e.g.* Paul Willis' *Learning to Labour* notes how the boys in his sample resisted both the *hidden curriculum* and teacher labelling.

respondent validation: the process by which the sociologist's interpretation of an event is checked with that of those who took part in the event.

response rate: the proportion of people selected to form a *sample* for a piece of research who respond either by returning a questionnaire or by agreeing to take part in an interview.

■ High response rates are necessary to ensure *representativeness*, although between 60 and 70% is acceptable. *Postal questionnaires*, however, may result in response rates of below 50%, which obviously undermines both their *reliability* and *validity*.

restricted code: a type of *language code*, identified by Basil Bernstein, characterised by short, grammatically correct, often unfinished sentences lacking in adverbs and adjectives, the meaning of which is often only understood by those who converse in it.

■ Bernstein argued that both the middle class and working class could converse in this code. However, the educational success of the middle class was due to their fluency in the *elaborated code* used in the educational system.

■ *TIP* Contrast the restricted and elaborated code in the context of *cultural deprivation theory* and *cultural capital* theory.

right-wing: any set of political ideas that are supportive of the status quo and especially capitalist enterprise, individual freedom and responsibility, traditional values and institutions, and minimal social change.

■ In terms of the political system, fascism is probably the most extreme of right-wing philosophies. The political right wing in the UK shifted from the paternal conservatism of the postwar *consensus* to the *New Right* ideas that underpinned Thatcher's period of office post-1979.

riot: see *urban riot*.

rite of passage: a ceremony or rituals that accompany a change in *status*, e.g. from child to adult, the emphasis on reaching the age of 18 or 21 in UK society, marriage etc.

role: a set of *norms* or patterns of behaviour that are culturally expected of a person or social group with a particular *status* or social position, e.g. doctors are expected by patients to maintain confidentiality and behave professionally.

■ Roles are also attached to *gender* characteristics. Society expects males and females to behave in particular ways which are learnt through *gender role socialisation*.

role conflict: the conflict of interests that sometimes arises out of the different *roles* one person has, e.g. the role of student may conflict with the role of part-time worker and negatively impact on academic study.

■ The media are fond of focusing on the alleged role conflict involved in being a working mother.

role model: a *significant other*, such as a parent, upon whom others, especially children, may model their own behaviour and attitudes.

RSA: see *repressive state apparatus*.

ruling class: defined by *elite theory* as the political governing class and by Marxists as the class that owns and controls the *means of production* and exploits the working class, thus ensuring monopoly over wealth and income, and cultural and political domination.

■ Marxists also use the terms *bourgeoisie* and capitalist class to describe this class.

sample: a group selected by the researcher from the *survey population* for study purposes.

▦ On the basis of findings from data gathered, the researchers make *generalisations* about the general population to which they belong.

sampling: the selection, usually in a scientific random systematic way, of a small representative group drawn from a larger survey population, who are invited to fill in *questionnaires* or take part in *interviews*.

▦ *Systematic* and *stratified sampling* are the two most common sampling methods used in sociological research, although sociologists have been known to use variations such as *quota sampling, multistage sampling* and *purposive sampling*, especially if no *sampling frame* is available. Non-random methods such as *snowball sampling* are sometimes used to obtain samples of groups that are unconventional or even deviant.

▦ *TIP* Sampling is an essential component of the *positivist* scientific approach because random sampling is thought to be *objective*.

sampling frame: a list of names such as those embodied by the *electoral register*, school rolls, telephone directories, list of employees in a company etc.

▦ Sometimes lists are unavailable and a map is used along with *multistage sampling*. Sometimes the sampling frame is identical to the *survey population*, e.g. the *census* is sent to every household in the UK. Sampling frames are sometimes problematic.

▦ *e.g.* The electoral register is probably best used shortly after it is compiled because people die or move away. However, not everyone is included — people may avoid registration to avoid paying council tax.

sampling unit: an individual, household or social group that is part of a *sampling frame* that a sociologist may sample as part of a wider survey population.

sanctions: rewards or punishments which reinforce socially expected behaviour that are an integral part of the *socialisation* process.

▦ Negative sanctions can be formal and take the form of capital punishment, imprisonment, fines etc. or they can be informal, e.g. the shunning of an individual by a social group.

science: literally meaning 'knowledge', it is normally used in commonsense terms to mean the 'natural sciences' of chemistry, physics and biology, which attempt to understand and explain the natural world in a systematic and logical manner (theory), by adopting specific techniques and procedures (method).

■ Science differs from other belief systems because it provides objective evidence for its propositions using logical and systematic means of collecting data. Other belief systems, such as commonsense and religion, depend upon faith or experience rather than fact. *Positivist* sociologists believe that sociology is a scientific discipline which can be used to predict human behaviour and uncover social laws that accurately describe the causes, functioning and consequences of phenomena. Over the years, positivists have developed a 'model' scientific approach to research, which is known as the *hypothetico-deductive approach*. However, not all sociologists accept that sociology is a science.

■ *e.g.* Popper is sceptical about the scientific status of sociology because he argues that it deals in theoretical concepts that are not open to *falsification*. Interpretivist sociology too is very sceptical and argues that the logic and methods of the natural sciences are inappropriate for sociology because the subject matter of sociology and the subject matter of the natural sciences are different. Human beings are active conscious beings, aware of what is going on in a social situation and capable of making choices about how to act. Natural phenomena, on the other hand, lack this consciousness.

■ *TIP* The issue of whether sociology is a science is part of a wider debate about how sociologists should study social behaviour between positivists and *anti-positivists*.

secondary data: second-hand data that might be used as part of sociological research in order to provide a historical and social context or even to form the central resource for analysis that has been published or written down.

■ Most sociologists embarking on research will take care to read previously published research.

■ *e.g.* It may take the form of *official statistics, historical documents, personal documents* such as letters, *diaries* etc.

secondary deviance: a term used by Edwin Lement that describes a person's response to society's definition of his or her activity as deviant or criminal.

■ The label of deviant or criminal becomes a *master status* that society uses to judge such individuals. Consequently, they may find it difficult to behave conventionally because society prevents them getting access to jobs etc. They may drift into a *subculture* of people similarly labelled and end up committing further crime, i.e. a *self-fulfilling prophecy*.

secondary labour market: that sector of employment in which jobs are mainly part-time, low-paid with less security and limited chances of promotion.

■ The secondary labour market is focused on by the *dual labour market theory*, which points out that it is dominated by females and members of ethnic minority groups in contrast with the *primary labour market*, which is dominated by white males.

S

secondary modern school: a type of school set up by the 1944 Education Act, which catered for those pupils who failed the *eleven-plus examination*.

■ These schools were supposed to experience 'parity of esteem' with the grammar schools in terms of resources, staffing and education. However, pupils, parents and employers generally saw them as second-class schools in contrast with the grammar schools. Most secondary schools were converted to comprehensive schools in the 1960s and 1970s, although they continue to exist in those areas which retained selective education.

secondary research: part of the sociological research process which involves reading other research in a particular field in order to inform potential *primary research* and to avoid unnecessary replication.

secondary socialisation: the wide range of social institutions and groups that transmit key cultural *values* and *norms* to children and adults, building upon and supplementing what has been learnt through *primary socialisation* in the family.

■ Education in the form of both the formal and *hidden curriculum, peer groups, religion* and *mass media* are the major agencies of secondary socialisation.

■ *TIP* It is sometimes argued that primary socialisation is becoming less important than secondary socialisation because family life is allegedly in decline.

second world: until the 1990s, a term used to describe communist/socialist societies such as the USSR, Czechoslovakia, East Germany, China, Cuba etc., in contrast with the free democracies of the *developed world*.

■ The collapse of the communist world — even China now has elements of free-market capitalism as part of its economic policy — has rendered the term largely obsolete.

sect: a religious group that may have broken away from an established religion (e.g. the Protestant religion began as a sect) or that represents an entirely new set of beliefs and practices.

■ Generally sects have no bureaucratic or hierarchical organisation, although they may have a leader with *charismatic authority* who claims to have a monopoly on truth. They have an exclusive membership in that they decide who should be recruited and members are expected to accept without question the barriers that exist between the sect and wider society. Members may, for example, have to give up contact with friends or family and change their name. Wilson distinguishes between *conversionist sects* and *introversionist sects*, whilst Wallis sees three types of sect — *world-affirming, world-accommodating* and *world-rejecting* — as making up new religious movements. Sociologists generally see sects emerging as the result of disillusion with the established church or as a reaction to the anxiety created by rapid social change or profound events like the millennium or as a reaction to *material* and/or social, *psychic, organismic* and *ethical deprivation*.

sectional groups: pressure groups that look after the interests of a particular section of the population.

■ *e.g.* Age Concern looks after the interests of the elderly.

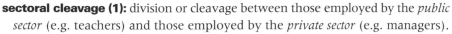

sectoral cleavage (1): division or cleavage between those employed by the *public sector* (e.g. teachers) and those employed by the *private sector* (e.g. managers).

■ These divisions or cleavages supposedly cut across traditional class allegiances to political parties, i.e. *partisan alignment*.

■ *e.g.* It is suggested that those employed by the public sector are more likely to vote for Labour, which tends to be in favour of 'tax and spend' policies. Saunders uses this idea to account for middle-class *deviant voters*, i.e. that sector of the middle class which votes Labour.

sectoral cleavage (2): the idea that there are significant differences in voting behaviour between those whose *consumption* depends on the *public sector* (e.g. council house tenants) and those who consume mainly through the *private sector* (e.g. owner occupiers, subscribers to private health schemes etc.).

■ *e.g.* It is suggested that those who are dependent on the state for income are more likely to vote for Labour, which tends to be in favour of a *welfare state*.

secular: not concerned with religion.

■ Modern societies are supposed to be secular societies based on rational thought and scientific endeavour in which people organise their lives around logical goals related to material rather than spiritual matters. However, evidence suggests that religion and quasi-religion still underpin belief systems and practices.

secularisation: defined by Bryan Wilson as the process whereby religious beliefs and practices lose social significance.

■ The debate about secularisation has proved problematic. There is little agreement among sociologists about how it ought to be measured. Wilson, for example, relied mainly on statistical evidence relating to church attendance and membership. However, such *secondary data* are regarded as both unreliable and potentially lacking in *validity* because, as Davie notes, belonging does not necessarily mean believing and vice versa. The major problem that underpins secularisation is that sociologists do not agree on how to define religion.

■ *e.g.* If religion is defined narrowly as participation in institutionalised religion, secularisation is probably occurring in the established churches, but evidence in regard to *sects*, *cults*, evangelical churches and ethnic minority religions indicates that religion is in good health. The extension of the definition of religion to include quasi-religious belief in things like fate, UFOs etc. and *surrogate religions*, such as devotion to a football team, further complicates and blurs the issue.

■ *TIP* Introducing secondary data in this debate is useful for illustrating the strengths and weaknesses of *official statistics* in a methods question.

segregated conjugal roles: domestic roles that are divided along traditional gender lines and carried out by husbands and wives, e.g. women doing the housework and looking after children whilst men do DIY, gardening and look after the car.

■ *Functionalist* thinkers have argued that such roles in the modern nuclear family are obsolete and have been replaced by *joint conjugal roles*, especially as women have entered the workforce in large numbers. However, there is little evidence to support this notion.

■ *e.g.* Surveys indicate that roles are still largely segregated along stereotypical lines and women now carry the *dual burden* of waged work and domestic labour.

selective benefit: a form of welfare benefit for which people must qualify because they fail to meet certain criteria in terms of adequate income, family supports etc.

■ People who apply for such benefits are often *means-tested*. The *New Right* is very keen on this type of benefit.

■ *e.g.* Income support.

selective exposure: an idea associated with the media sociologist Klapper, which states that before media content can have any effect, people must choose to access it and this depends on a range of influences including parental control, education, interest etc.

■ *e.g.* Klapper notes that people tend to choose programmes that confirm their existing tastes, values and prejudices and they are generally not interested in programmes that aim to change their beliefs or behaviour.

■ *TIP* Use as a critique of theories of *media effects*, which suggest media content directly affects people's beliefs and behaviour.

selective perception: once exposed to media content, Klapper notes that people interpret it in different ways and may well choose to ignore its messages.

■ *TIP* Use this concept alongside *selective exposure* and *selective retention*.

selective retention: In regard to media content, Klapper notes that people only remember that which supports their beliefs.

■ Klapper's theory of *selective exposure, selective perception* and selective retention suggests that social behaviour is more complex than that found in the hypodermic syringe approach to media effects. Klapper argues that what the media do to the audience is less important than what audiences do with the media.

self: an individual's subjective sense of his or her own *identity*.

■ This is partly a product of what others expect (e.g. a mother may see herself as a good mother because she achieves society's standards in this respect) and partly how a person interprets his or her experience of other people's reactions to them (e.g. some mothers, despite being good mothers, may be criticised for working). The self is the connection between society and the individual, because people judge themselves (as do others) on whether they are living up to the social norms expected of particular social *roles*.

self-estrangement: an aspect of *alienation* at work, identified by Blauner, along with isolation, *powerlessness* and *meaninglessness*, that refers to workers being unable to express themselves through their work or to feel involved in it.

■ Blauner found high self-estrangement in industries characterised by machine technology and especially assembly-line production.

self-fulfilling prophecy: situations in which the positive and negative behaviour of individuals is shaped by the imposition of labels by powerful groups such as teachers and police officers.

■ The idea originated with Rosenthal and Jacobsen's *Pygmalion in the Classroom* and has come to be used extensively by *labelling theory* in explaining under-achievement by focusing on *teacher expectations* and labelling, and how these are conveyed to children during *classroom interaction*. However, the concept is speculative rather than based on hard empirical evidence. It is also implicitly *over-deterministic*, because it implies that once negatively labelled, pupils experience a downward spiral into failure. It neglects the possibility of pupil negotiation and *resistance*.

■ *TIP* An important concept but be able to evaluate it.

self-identity: see *self*.

self-reports: a method of research used by sociologists working in the field of crime and deviance consisting of confidential *questionnaires* that ask respondents voluntarily to record whether they have committed any of the offences listed.

■ Self-reporting suggests that criminal activity is more common and spread out more evenly across the population than *official statistics* indicate. In particular, self-reports indicate that crime committed by females and middle-class males is likely to go under-reported and therefore undetected. However, the *validity* of self-reports has been questioned.

■ *e.g.* People, especially youth, may exaggerate, lie or understate their involvement in what respondents may regard as a sensitive and loaded field of enquiry. Moreover, self-reports rarely include serious crime on their lists.

semiology: the analysis of signs such as those contained within language or images in advertisements in order to understand the hidden ideological messages and assumptions that lie beneath the surface.

■ Sociologists distinguish between what is denoted or actually shown and connotation, i.e. the implicit meaning of the image or text. For example, the opening credits of James Bond films denote scantily clad females and guns, which connote sex, glamour and action. Semiotic analysis produces *qualitative data* but is criticised by *positivists* because it lacks the scientific characteristics of a method such as the *social survey*.

■ *e.g.* It is heavily dependent upon the selective interpretations of the researcher. There is no guarantee that other members share the same interpretations.

serial monogamy: a growing trend in modern Britain because of divorce and remarriage, whereby people can expect to have two or three long-term monogamous relationships resulting in cohabitation or marriage during their lifetime.

service class: the term used by the *Oxford mobility study* to mean RG social class I (higher-grade professionals) and RG social class II (lower-grade professionals).

■ The occupational scale used by the Oxford study is very similar to that adopted by the *NS–SEC*.

S

sex: the biological and physiological differences between males and females, e.g. genitalia, often contrasted with the social category of *gender*.

sexism: *prejudice* and *discrimination* that are practised against women because of their *sex* and *gender*, which derive from and maintain the forces of *patriarchy*.

sex stereotyping: see *gender stereotyping*.

sexual division of labour: the division of both paid work and domestic labour into men's jobs and women's jobs.

■ In terms of employment, sociologists have suggested that the sexual division of labour is characterised by *vertical* and *horizontal segregation*. Moreover, there is evidence that few women question the division of labour in the home, in which they are still primarily responsible for childcare and housework, despite holding down full-time jobs.

sick role: the rights, responsibilities and behaviour associated with being sick and being unable to perform a social role.

■ Parsons notes that the ill person is exempt from responsibilities such as work but suggests that they have a responsibility themselves to seek professional help and be seen to be attempting to get well.

■ *e.g.* The role of doctors is to act as agents of social control, i.e. to confirm the sick role officially in order to maintain responsibility amongst the ill and to encourage their swift return to their social roles and obligations.

sign: an aspect of culture such as language, images, stories, clothing, food etc. that has cultural meaning for social actors, which can be accessed and understood through the use of *semiology*.

significant other: influential person who may be adopted as a *role model*, especially during the *primary socialisation* period, e.g. parents.

■ *Self*-identity develops when children develop the ability to be able to take on the role of significant others, e.g. during games, and therefore begin to see and understand how others see them.

single-parent family: see *one-parent family*.

sink estate: a deprived council estate to which councils allocate so-called problem families, e.g. *one-parent families*, drug-users, community care patients etc.

■ Such estates may be labelled by the local authority, police and media as 'problem estates' and consequently little public money may be spent on the upkeep of the housing stock or local facilities.

■ *e.g.* Such estates often acquire a catalogue of problems such as high rates of burglary, vandalism, car-crime, drug-taking, suicide, depression etc.

sink school: a school that appears to be doing badly according to *league tables* of test results and that consequently finds it difficult with open enrolment to attract children and parents.

■ Such schools may be providing an effective learning experience for low-ability pupils, but league tables do not assess this strength. Consequently, parents may not want to send their children to such schools. Rolls may fall and such schools face closure. In some cases the government has appointed super-heads to sort these schools out.

situational constraints: an explanation for poverty which suggests that the behaviour of the poor is a consequence of the material constraints in their lives, e.g. lack of money, jobs, education, opportunities etc., over which they have little control, rather than the result of a deficient culture.

■ Surveys of the poor support this idea because they show that the poor generally share the same aspirations as mainstream society.

■ *TIP* The idea of situational constraints is often used as a critique of both the *culture of poverty* and *underclass* theories.

skills: a set of abilities and techniques, which can be manual or mental, that are usually learned in Western societies through schooling and/or training and are usually measured through the use of tests and examinations and the acquisition of qualifications.

■ *Functionalist* sociologists see a close relationship between skills, the economy and *stratification*, whilst the *New Right* have been concerned that education has not paid enough attention to vocational skills in the past. The *new vocationalism* was a direct result of that concern. Marxist sociologists such as Braverman argue that skill in modern societies is less important today and that some occupations, especially white-collar jobs, are consequently experiencing *deskilling*.

snowball sampling: a method of compiling a *sample* of a social group by contacting one member of a group who may introduce the researcher to other members.

■ This type of non-random sampling tends to occur when the social group is deviant or unconventional and may not be interested in volunteering itself for sociological study. However, the researcher can never be sure that the group contacted is *representative* of the wider research population.

■ *e.g.* Parker used this type of sampling for his study of heroin users in the Wirrall.

social action theory: also known as *interpretive sociology*, this theory takes a *micro* approach to explaining and understanding human behaviour and stresses the ability of individuals to exert control over their own actions.

■ The individual is not seen as a passive recipient of society's directions but as an active creator of social behaviour. Social action theory rejects the positivist view that society has an independent existence or objective reality and that social situations are the product of structural factors, and argues that social reality is the outcome of human beings making choices to engage in interaction with each other and the shared interpretations or meanings we bring to those interactions.

social administrative theory: a theory of health inequalities which suggests that these are largely caused by inequalities in the distribution of NHS resources as symbolised by the *inverse care law*.

S

■ It also points out that the NHS often ignores the health needs of ethnic minorities by failing to produce health information in appropriate languages, and by not making knowledge of religious, dietary and cultural norms part of health professional training.

social change: generally, the difference between societies and social institutions as they once were and how they are today, i.e. the transition from the traditional to the modern.

■ Explaining social change has been a major concern of sociology. The early *classical sociologists* were concerned with explaining the change from *preindustrial society* to modern industrial society and how the changes brought about by *industrialisation*, technology and *urbanisation* have affected the organisation of society and social life.

■ *e.g.* Durkheim focused on the change from societies based on *mechanical solidarity* to societies based on *organic solidarity*, whilst Marx traced the history of class struggle from 'primitive communism' through slave and *feudal* societies to *capitalism*. Recently sociology has focused on the possibility that industrial societies may have developed into *postindustrial* or postcapitalist societies. Moreover, *postmodernists* suggested that *modernity* is dissolving and being replaced by a new type of postmodern social order in which the classic sociological theories are increasingly irrelevant.

social class: a system of *stratification* found in modern industrial societies, consisting of three broad groups of people (i.e. *upper class, middle class* and *working class*) who share similar economic positions in terms of occupation, income, ownership of wealth and probably similar levels of education, status and lifestyle.

■ Social class systems differ from *feudal* or *caste* systems of stratification because they are open *meritocratic* societies, i.e. people can experience upward or downward *social mobility* as they acquire or lose jobs, although mobility is also possible through marriage and the acquisition of wealth. Social class is central to the Marxist theory of society.

■ *e.g.* Marxists define a person's class in terms of their proximity to the *means of production*. The capitalist class or *bourgeoisie* own the means of production and hire and exploit the *labour power* of the working class. Marxists claim that social class therefore is the source of all social inequality. Other sociologists criticise Marxists for neglecting other important sources of inequality such as gender and ethnicity. Social class is measured today by the *NS–SEC*. There is strong evidence that social class is still very influential today as illustrated by class inequalities in *mortality* and *morbidity rates*, educational achievement and the distribution of wealth and poverty.

social closure: the ability of the *upper class* to close themselves off from lower socioeconomic groups and so deny upward *social mobility* into their ranks.

■ They do this by controlling entry into elite institutions such as the top public schools, exclusive gentlemen's clubs and occupations such as merchant banking

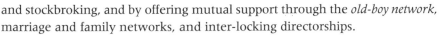

and stockbroking, and by offering mutual support through the *old-boy network*, marriage and family networks, and inter-locking directorships.

social construction: behaviour that is thought of as natural or as fact but that is actually the product of cultural expectations and processes.

■ *Official statistics* on crime are thought by many to be a scientific indicator of the degree of criminal behaviour in society. However, sociologists point out that they are a social construction in that they are the end-product of a social collection process involving the interpretations of victims, the police and the courts.

■ *e.g.* Criminal statistics may tell us more about the people who collected them than about crime and criminality. Moreover, our definitions of what counts as crime are also socially constructed, since definitions of what constitutes crime differ across societies and even within societies, i.e. many young people do not see soft drug use as criminal but it is socially constructed as such by the law.

■ *TIP* Suicide and *gender* are two 'facts' that are also socially constructed.

social consumption: see *consumption*.

social control: the process of persuading, encouraging and enforcing *conformity* to cultural *values* and *norms*.

■ This is a crucial part of the *primary socialisation* process in the family, which usually involves the development of a conscience in the child via role-playing and the use of informal *sanctions*. Social control is also enforced by agents of *secondary socialisation* such as schools. *Agents of social control* such as police and courts use formal sanctions to punish those who fail to conform and commit crime. Functionalists see socialisation and social control as ensuring *value consensus* and *social order* whilst Marxists argue that social control is about conformity to the capitalist order and consequently is aimed at controlling the revolutionary potential of the working class.

social democrat: an approach to the economy and *welfare state* which believes that government intervention is all-important, to make sure that inequalities between people do not become too great.

■ Social democrats believe that the free market benefits the rich and harms the poor so there is a need for government regulation of the economy at the very least. Social democrats therefore believe that all citizens should have the right to vote, the right justice under the law and the right to universal and comprehensive welfare benefits. They believe that the welfare state should be the central defining institution of the modern state. One drawback of this model is the high cost of the welfare state.

social desirability effect: a methodological problem of *validity* that arises out of respondents, especially in interview situations, wanting to please or impress the researcher.

■ It involves the over-reporting of 'desirable' things such as giving to charity, voting or obeying the law, and the under-reporting of 'undesirable' things such as illness, disability, alcohol consumption, racist behaviour etc.

S

social experiment: see *field experiment.*

social facts: a term used by Durkheim to describe the external social phenomena, i.e. social laws, that allegedly constrain human behaviour.

■ In his theory of *egoistic suicide* Durkheim concluded that a person's potential to commit this type of suicide was increased if society experienced excessive individualism, i.e. if people were not sufficiently integrated into society. In this case *individualism* and *social integration* were social facts influencing individual behaviour and, according to Durkheim, could be studied as 'things'.

social inequality: unequal opportunities or rewards experienced by individuals or groups, especially the working class, ethnic minorities and females.

■ *Critical sociologists* such as Marxists and feminists see modern societies as characterised by class and gender inequalities respectively. Marxists see social inequalities as rooted in the organisation of *capitalism*, whilst feminists see it arising out of the *patriarchy* that characterises society. Other sociologists see ethnic inequalities as rooted in *institutional racism*. Functionalists, on the other hand, argue that social inequality is a natural outcome of *meritocracies* and has a beneficial effect on society in that it motivates people to improve their position in society.

social integration: a sense of belonging to a particular social group, community or society.

■ *Functionalists* believe that a vital function of the education system is to integrate new members of society into the existing culture.

■ *e.g.* The teaching of history is a key means of achieving this goal because it celebrates the achievements of society and promotes pride and a sense of community.

socialisation: an ongoing process whereby individuals learn to conform to cultural values and norms and acquire the social expectations attached to particular roles mainly through the family (i.e. *primary socialisation*) and through contact with education, religion, work, mass media, peer group etc. (i.e. *secondary socialisation*).

socialism: a set of political ideas that stress the social or shared ownership of the *means of production* through the state and the redistribution of income and wealth to the working class in order to achieve an *egalitarian* society.

■ From time to time, socialist ideas have had an influence on Labour Party policy, especially in its commitment until the 1980s to public ownership in the form of *nationalisation* of key industries. However, in April 1995 the Labour Party voted to repeal Clause 4 of the Party Constitution, which advocated common ownership of the means of production.

social mobility: movement of individuals or groups up and down the class system as measured by movement within their lifetime (i.e. *intragenerational mobility*) or by contrast with their parents (*intergenerational mobility*).

■ *Functionalists* and *New Right* thinkers argue that the study of social mobility is important because evidence should show that the UK is an open society or *meritocracy. Critical sociologists* suggest that mobility studies show that meritocracy is a myth. Evidence from the major study of social mobility, i.e. the *Oxford mobility study*, tends to support both positions in that it shows increases in the *absolute rate of mobility* but class inequalities in the *relative rate of mobility*, i.e. the *1.2.4. rule of relative hope*.

social model of health: a theory associated with McKeown which points out that health levels as measured by increases in life expectancy and improvements in child mortality had dramatically improved before the development of modern biomedical techniques such as vaccination.

■ McKeown argues that nineteenth-century public health measures, e.g. sewage systems, clean water supplies etc., and improvements in nutrition and diet and birth limitation are mainly responsible for good health today.

social order: from a *functionalist* perspective the stability, *social solidarity* and *social integration* that derive from shared *norms* and *values* (*value consensus*) and the inter-dependence of skills found in the modern *division of labour*.

■ Functionalism focuses on explaining how social order originates and how it is maintained by social institutions such as the family, education, law, mass media, religion etc. which function to socialise society's members into consensus and regulate their behaviour.

■ *e.g.* Some of these institutions, such as education and work, aim to equip people with the *skills* required so that their abilities are identified and used in ways that make an effective and efficient contribution to the economy. However, functionalism is especially criticised by Marxists, who see society as characterised by *class conflict* rather than social order.

social policy: government ideas, plans and legislation aimed at meeting the social needs of the population. For example, the *welfare state* is a collection of social policies, e.g. health, social security etc., that aims to maintain welfare.

■ There is a strong connection between social policy and sociology. Sociological research has contributed to social policy in the fields of education, poverty, religion etc. However, some sociologists, mainly functionalists, suggest that sociology should subscribe to '*objectivity* through neutrality'. It was argued that it is the job of the researcher to carry out research objectively, and that the way in which the research data are used by social policy-makers is not the business of sociologists.

■ *e.g.* The job of sociologists is not to solve social problems or change society. However, *critical sociologists* such as Marxists and feminists believe that sociology should be prescriptive and encourage social policy in order to relieve social inequalities such as child poverty.

social problem: social behaviour that causes public conflict and/or private misery and results in collective action, e.g. social policy, legislation, social controls etc., to solve it.

■ Social problems are a relative concept and their definition will depend on factors such as culture, place, time and social context.

S

■ *e.g.* Many people on the right of the political spectrum see ethnic minorities as a social problem whereas liberals may regard *racism* as a social problem.

social science: a collection of academic disciplines that focus on the systematic and scientific study of society, social phenomena and human behaviour and usually include psychology, economics and sociology, although the status of the latter is seen by some as problematic.

■ *Positivists* are keen for sociology to be defined as a science whereas *interpretivist* sociologists do not see this qualification as strictly necessary in order to carry out effective research.

■ *TIP* The 'Is sociology a science?' debate revolves around how science is defined and how positivists and interpretivists explain social behaviour.

social solidarity: the unification of diverse groups so that they feel a common sense of mutual interests, *community, social integration* and a strong sense of belonging to a particular society.

■ *Functionalists* argue that education functions to bring about social solidarity through the teaching of common history, language etc.

■ *e.g.* Durkheim focused on how social change involved a movement from societies based on *mechanical solidarity* to societies based on *organic solidarity*. He also noted that any lessening in social integration, which he saw mainly as the product of controls associated with religion and family life, would result in social conditions in which excessive *individualism* could thrive, leading to increases in *egoistic suicide*.

social status: see *status*.

social structure: generally, the way a society is organised in terms of social institutions, processes and relationships.

■ Sociological theories of social structure (i.e. *structuralism*) see human behaviour as constrained and even determined by social structures over which individuals have little or no control.

social survey: a method that normally involves the random selection of a representative sample from a research population, administering *questionnaires* and/or conducting *structured interviews*.

■ This is the research method thought to be most scientific and consequently most favoured by positivist sociologists.

■ *e.g.* All questions are standardised and all respondents are exposed to the same stimuli. It is objective in that random sampling techniques should minimise possible *bias*. It is reliable in that the results should not be affected by the person who administers the questionnaire or conducts the interview. It results in large amounts of *quantitative data* in a relatively short period of time, although some surveys are *longitudinal*.

society: a social group that occupies a particular geographical territory and shares a sense of belonging to a common culture and set of institutions.

■ A society is not the same as a *nation state*. For example, the United Kingdom is a nation state but it contains several societies, e.g. Welsh, Scottish, Jewish,

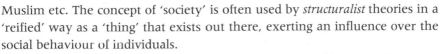

Muslim etc. The concept of 'society' is often used by *structuralist* theories in a 'reified' way as a 'thing' that exists out there, exerting an influence over the social behaviour of individuals.

sociobiology: the view that all social behaviour is directed by natural instincts or biological drives, in particular the drive to survive and reproduce.

■ Wilson explains human sexual behaviour in these terms. He claims that men are more promiscuous than women because during the female's lifetime she only has a limited number of chances to have children. She is more interested in *monogamy* because that relationship is likely to ensure that her few children survive. Males, on the other hand, can potentially father as many children as they want with many women. They are therefore more interested in promiscuity. However, in criticism of these ideas, sociologists point to the diversity of human culture with regard to sexual behaviour. Sociologists claim culture and environment are more influential than biology.

socioeconomic group: the classification of individuals into occupational groups which tend to be similar in income, lifestyle, education and status, as used in the *Registrar-General's classification of occupations* and the *NS–SEC*.

■ Such socioeconomic groups are often referred to as *social classes*.

sociolinguistics: the study of the social and cultural origins and use of language.

■ Sociologists have studied the role of language in gender and ethnic inequalities in education but sociolinguistics is mainly associated with Bernstein's attempt to relate *language codes* to social class in his identification of *restricted* and *elaborated codes*.

sociological problem: any pattern or trend in social relationships that calls for an explanation.

■ For example, divorce is a sociological problem because its patterns indicate the importance of variables such as length of marriage etc.

sociology: the study of human social life, groups and societies that encompasses encounters between individuals on a one-to-one basis and the investigation of worldwide social processes.

■ There are three points of difference between sociology and commonsense everyday experience. First, sociology is systematic in that it involves established rules of investigation that aim to produce an *objective* or neutral view of the social world. Second, it is based on factual evidence that can be checked and evaluated by other sociologists. Third, sociology is critical in that sociologists adopt a kind of rigorous scepticism about social life.

stabilisation of adult personality: a key function of the family and specifically the female *expressive role*, according to *functionalist* sociology, is the stabilisation of the male adult personality.

■ Functionalists like Parsons argued that the male *instrumental leader* experiences the outside world as stressful and therefore needs to be emotionally stabilised through play with children and through the emotional and sexual supports offered by females.

state: the central political authority that rules over a given territory, which includes a legislature that passes laws, an executive government that carries out the will of the legislature, a bureaucracy, a judiciary and a military machine.

■ Until the twentieth century, the state was reluctant to interfere in the lives of its citizens but since the Second World War it has assumed responsibility for the management of the economy and the welfare of its citizens. *Pluralists* see the role of the state as an honest broker that regulates competing *pressure groups* and operates to make sure no one group accumulates too much political power. *Instrumental Marxists* see it as an instrument of the ruling class, whilst *hegemonic Marxists* see it as relatively autonomous from the ruling class but benefiting that class because the state manages capitalism via economic policy.

status: the *prestige* or social esteem attached to a particular role by society, which may be used as a type of social ranking or the basis for a *stratification* system.

■ It is usually based on education and lifestyle and consequently it confers positive and negative privileges on people, depending on whether or not they have these social attributes.

■ *e.g.* In the *apartheid* system that existed in South Africa, status or lack of it depended on colour of skin, whilst in the Indian *caste system* it depends upon religious 'purity'. Sociologists argue that status is generally *ascribed* in preindustrial and non-industrial societies, whilst it is achieved in modern capitalist societies.

status frustration: the idea that some social groups, particularly working-class and ethnic minority youth, may be denied *status* in education and may react in frustration by forming *delinquent subcultures* whose members award status to each other on the basis of carrying out anti-school activities.

■ This idea is also present in the *left realist* theory of crime. Young and Lea focus on the *relative deprivation* and *powerlessness* of youth in the inner cities and note that their frustration may boil over into *urban riots*, crime etc.

stereotyping: generally, the negative labelling of a whole group that is based on over-simplified, exaggerated and often mistaken generalisations which make clear that group's subordinate position.

■ Stereotyping is essentially *prejudice*, an expression of ideological values which creates and reinforces social divisions between groups, i.e. 'them versus us'. It is generally aimed at groups that lack power, e.g. women, ethnic minorities, the elderly, youth *subcultures* etc., and may be used to justify *discrimination* against such groups.

stratification: the division of society into a pattern of layers or strata made up of a hierarchy of unequal social groups based on factors such as wealth and income, occupation and status, *social class*, political power, religion, race, gender and age.

■ Sociologists have identified four main types of stratification system: *feudalism*, *apartheid*, *caste* and social class.

■ *e.g.* The sociology of stratification mainly focuses on systems found in modern societies which are generally based on inequalities relating to social class, especially in terms of wealth, income, poverty, employment, education and health. In recent years, ethnic, gender and age systems of stratification have become increasingly important in studying inequality.

stratified sampling: a sampling method in which the *sampling frame* is divided into strata, e.g. into males and females, age groups etc., and a random sample is chosen from each category.

streaming: the separation of pupils in schools into different ability groups.

■ Studies have demonstrated a clear relationship between social class and allocations to streams across the educational system. Evidence suggests that middle-class children dominate top streams and that children with unskilled manual parents are over-proportionately found in bottom streams. *Symbolic interactionists* view streaming as a form of institutionalised *labelling* in which top streams are composed of middle-class *ideal pupils* and bottom streams composed of problematic working-class and ethnic minority children.

■ *e.g.* It is suggested that streaming results in teachers transmitting different types of knowledge and skills to each stream (i.e. academic to the top streams and vocational to the bottom). Bottom streams may react by forming *counter-school cultures* which result in a *self-fulfilling prophecy* and confirm *teacher expectations*.

■ *TIP* The work of the *Marxist phenomenologist* Paul Willis is critical of this symbolic interactionist position.

street crime: crime such as robbery, mugging and violence, which is more likely to be carried out by lower-class youth and which is subject to greater amounts of public intolerance, media complaint, criminal law and policing than other offences.

■ Some explanations of street crime suggest that the *official statistics* are exaggerated by the over-policing of these crimes and the attention paid to them by media *moral panics*. Marxist writers suggest that such crimes are a form of political protest against the *alienation* and deprivation of capitalist society. *Left realism* suggests that this type of crime needs to be taken seriously because it is a serious problem within inner-city areas.

strike: a form of industrial action that involves the temporary and usually official (i.e. sanctioned by a trade union) and unofficial withdrawal of labour in order to express a grievance or make a demand.

■ Britain acquired an international reputation in the 1970s as a strike-prone nation but the facts of the last 20 years suggest that strikes are relatively rare in the UK. Explanations for strikes once mainly focused on the *proletarian traditionalist* working class and their strong sense of *identity*, who saw society in terms of 'us versus them', i.e. management. However, most strikes today focus on wage disputes and the reorganisation of the workplace, which usually results in redundancy and a relative lowering of wages. This supports the view that workers today are *instrumental collectivist* in orientation.

structural differentiation: the development of specialised agencies following *industrialisation* that took over many of the functions traditionally performed by the family and religion in *preindustrial society*.

■ The idea is associated with Parsons, who saw the preindustrial *extended family* as a multifunctional unit responsible for production of food, shelter and clothing, whilst family and religion provided education, health care, welfare etc. After industrialisation the family lost the production function to factories and family members became wage-earners. The state eventually took over education, health and welfare from the family and the church. This has allowed both the family and religion to specialise in socialisation into culture and morality respectively.

structuralism: theories that see human behaviour as constrained and even shaped by the social organisation of society, i.e. the *social structure*, made up of inter-related institutions such as families, schools, religions, the economy, the political system etc.

■ Such theories suggest that people are the puppets of society and that sociologists should focus on studying the effects of social structure on social life. Both functionalism and Marxism are structural theories.

■ *e.g.* Functionalism sees human behaviour as the result of *value consensus*, which means that people generally share the same values and norms and consequently their actions are patterned and predictable. Marxism sees human behaviour as the product of class inequality and conflict that underpins the organisation of capitalist societies. The critique of structuralism mainly comes from *interpretive sociology*.

■ *TIP* It is important to understand the similarities between functionalism and Marxism as well as their differences.

structurally isolated nuclear family: see *relative isolation of the family*.

structural Marxism: a theoretical approach which suggests that economic and social inequalities are the natural product of the structural organisation of capitalism rather than the product of deliberate strategies by the bourgeoisie or capitalist class.

■ In the field of political sociology, Poulantzas notes that it would not matter what political party exercised power because if capitalism is not dismantled, the capitalist class will always benefit from its management. In the field of media sociology, structuralist Marxists have made an important contribution to the debate on ownership and control of the media, especially regarding why media content often seems to support capitalist interests. It is claimed that this is an accidental by-product of the social backgrounds of journalists/editors, and the need to attract the largest possible audience in order to enhance profits. Marxists point out that journalists are recruited from a very narrow social background, i.e. middle-class, white and male. They therefore subscribe to *news values* that stress a worldview of consensus and consequently avoid or trivialise extreme ideas in order not to lose their audience. This theory is generally critical of the *instrumental Marxist* theory of media, which sees news as shaped by a deliberate conspiracy by owners etc.

structuration: a theory originating with Giddens that attempts to combine structure and action by suggesting that people interpret the world around them and make choices on how they should react and behave, but those choices are constrained and shaped by the organisation or structure of the society in which they live.

■ Individuals react to external forces such as the limitations of coming from certain social backgrounds in a variety of ways.

■ *e.g.* Some will choose to negotiate a path through the obstacles that a discriminatory society throws up whilst others will choose a path of complete *resistance*. However, some individuals will find that whatever their interpretation and response to structural pressures, their choices will be limited or partially shaped by the structure of their society.

structure: see *social structure*.

structured interview: a formal interview, commonly used in *social surveys*, in which a trained interviewer asks all respondents taking part the same standardised questions from a prepared *questionnaire* or *interview schedule*.

■ The uniformity of the questionnaire, which generally uses *closed questions*, is aimed at the collection of reliable *qualitative data*. Moreover, the distance between the interviewer and the respondent (i.e. there is no personal relationship as such) is aimed at maintaining *objectivity*. This method is therefore regarded by *positivist* sociologists as having all the characteristics required of an effective scientific approach.

subculture: a social group who subscribe to the *values* and *norms* of mainstream society in most respects but may support some norms and values that are distinct from society and generally regarded as deviant.

■ A range of sociological theories have focused on the role of subcultures, as sources both of deviant and criminal behaviour and of educational underachievement.

■ *e.g.* British Marxists have focused on deviant youth subcultures such as skinheads, mods and punks and explained their behaviour as a form of temporary and magical resistance to aspects of capitalism. American subcultural theory focused on how the deficiencies of working-class culture and the failure of institutions to provide working-class boys with status led to subcultures that awarded status to members on the basis of delinquent activities. These ideas were taken up by *symbolic interactionist* studies of education, which saw subcultures as a reaction to labelling and *streaming*. Lately, *left realism* has focused on the role of subcultures in *street crime* whilst there has recently been interest in how male subcultures in schools may be contributing to *male underachievement*.

subjective social class: the social class that people feel themselves to be in, which may clash with the objective measurements of class used by both the *Registrar-General* and *NS–SEC*.

S

subjectivity: the extent to which the personal opinions, experiences and *biases* of the sociologist affect the design and outcome of research.

▧ *Positivists* view subjectivity as unscientific and undesirable and champion *objectivity*. *Interpretivists* argue that objectivity is not of central importance because it is only by subjectively identifying with the individual or situation being investigated that a true interpretation of what is going on can be obtained.

subsistence poverty: see *absolute poverty*.

subterranean values: a concept associated with Matza who suggests that all members of society subscribe to 'deviant' values such as craving excitement, enjoying aggression, acting on the spur of the moment etc.

▧ Matza notes that most members of society express these values in a socially acceptable fashion through leisure activities, e.g. playing sport, watching a film etc. Delinquents express these values in the wrong place and at the wrong time, e.g. at school, in front of police officers etc. Matza is therefore suggesting that normal and deviant behaviour originate in the same set of values.

suicide: the intentional taking of one's own life.

▧ This subject became the theoretical battleground of the *positivist* versus *interpretivist* debate when Durkheim argued that the suicide rate was socially determined by the organisation of societies and especially the degree or level of *social integration* and *moral regulation* that existed in societies. However, interpretivist sociologists argue that suicide rates are *social constructions* in that they reflect the different cultural meanings attached to suicide in particular societies.

▧ *e.g.* Douglas points out that the suicide rate is high in Japan because suicide is regarded as an honourable activity whilst it is low in Catholic societies because suicide is regarded as a cardinal sin and covered up by family and officials. Moreover, a death is not a suicide until officially labelled as such by coroners, whose interpretation of the same evidence may result in quite different verdicts.

superclass: defined by Adonis and Pollard as a *socioeconomic group* that appeared during the 1980s, composed of members of the old professions (especially law) who made their fortunes in the City, accountants and managers of investment funds and directors of former public utilities (e.g. water, gas, railways etc.), who have more in common with the *upper class* than the middle class.

▧ This superclass earn astronomical salaries. The media refer to them as 'fat-cats'.

▧ *e.g.* They can be distinguished from the rest of society by their *consumption* patterns, which revolve around nannies and servants, second homes, exotic holidays, private health and pension schemes and private education for their children. Most of the superclass live and work in London and the southeast.

superstructure: according to Marxism, the social institutions such as the family, education, mass media, religion etc. that function to transmit ruling-class *ideology* and therefore reproduce, maintain and legitimate class inequality.

▧ According to Marxists such as Althusser, this *ideological state apparatus* is extremely successful in making sure that the working class are unaware of the conflicts of interest that divide them from the capitalist class.

■ *e.g.* The *hidden curriculum* ensures that working-class pupils blame themselves for their educational failure rather than an educational system organised primarily to benefit middle-class pupils. The true nature of capitalist exploitation of the working class therefore goes unrecognised and this *false consciousness* ensures that inequality is accepted as natural and inevitable, and working-class conformity and class inequalities are reproduced generation by generation. The superstructure is therefore determined by the economic relationships of class inequality that underpin the *infrastructure*.

surplus value: the difference between the value of labour when sold as a product and the wage paid by the capitalist for that labour, which Marxists see as the root cause of the great inequalities of wealth and income between the working class and the ruling class.

surrogate religion: institutions and beliefs that function like a religion in maintaining *social integration* and *social solidarity*, e.g. nationalism, communism, sport etc., through religion-like rituals.

■ Coles notes that going to a football match resembles religion in that it comprises large numbers of people with a common purpose and involves sacred symbols, e.g. shirts, flags and powerful emotions. Football may therefore be a surrogate religion.

survey: see *social survey*.

survey population: the population that is the subject of the research.

■ A *sample* of this population will be asked to fill in a questionnaire or take part in an interview.

symbolic annihilation: the fact that women and minorities such as gays and lesbians and the elderly appear less often than men on television and when they do, they are often represented in a limited way as *stereotypes* and their activities trivialised or condemned.

symbolic interactionism: a theory within *interpretive sociology* which aims to show that people make choices and act purposefully as a result of the sharing of symbols. They are thus able to make sense of the interactions that make up their social world.

■ Like other interpretivist approaches, symbolic interactionists have tended to focus on *micro-sociological* processes such as teacher–pupil and police officer–suspect interactions using *observation* techniques. Consequently, symbolic interactionism has made a significant contribution to our understanding of *classroom interaction* and especially the effect of *teacher expectations,* labelling and the *self-fulfilling prophecy* on educational underachievement. It has also highlighted the relativity of *deviance* and the role of power differences in defining what constitutes crime and deviance.

symmetrical family: a type of home-centred *nuclear family* identified by Wilmott and Young in the early 1970s that was particularly characterised by *joint conjugal roles*, i.e. husbands and wives allegedly became more alike and equal.

■ Wilmott and Young suggested that the movement of women into the workforce had been paralleled by men taking more responsibility for childcare and housework. Whilst there is some evidence that men have increased their participation in childcare, dozens of empirical studies indicate that men's contribution to the *domestic division of labour* is far from equal.

systematic sampling: the most common type of sampling method, which involves taking a series of names from a *sampling frame* at randomly chosen intervals.

■ *e.g.* Out of a group of 500 people, 50 may be chosen by randomly selecting a number between 1 and 10, e.g. 6. Starting with 6, every tenth name from the sampling frame, i.e. 6, 16, 26, 36 and so on, is selected as the sample.

target-hardening: an anti-crime strategy popular with *control theory* which suggests that the targets of crime should be made harder to remove or vandalise.

▓ Control theory research focused on analysing how criminals identify targets in order to increase the costs of crime, especially the chances of being caught. More effective security devices, especially surveillance cameras in city centres, property identity marking and better street security and lighting, are all seen as effective forms of target hardening.

Taylorism: the putting into practice of F. W. Taylor's scientific management theory, whereby the labour process is broken down into its simplest parts and management controls the pace of the work, as on the assembly line.

▓ Marxists such as Braverman see this process as the beginning of *deskilling*.

teacher expectations: a set of assumptions held by some teachers supposedly in regard to pupil ability, but thought by *interactionist* sociologists to be connected to *stereotypes* held about the aptitude of pupils from working-class backgrounds and female and ethnic minority pupils.

▓ It is argued that teacher expectations may evolve from an *ideal pupil* stereotype which sees middle-class pupils as suited to academic work.

▓ *e.g.* Pupils who do not fit this stereotype may be negatively labelled and the label communicated via *classroom interaction*. A *self-fulfilling prophecy* may come about as a result of a decline in pupils' self-esteem.

tertiary sector: otherwise known as the service sector, the part of the economy that is based on the provision of services and is supposed to dominate post-industrial society.

Thatcherism: a type of *New Right* ideology dominant in the Conservative Party during the premiership of Margaret Thatcher and embodied by her which preached minimal state intervention and the promotion of free enterprise and individual choice.

▓ In terms of social policy, it was symbolised by her determination to challenge the power of organisations such as the trade unions, to privatise state-owned utilities, the selling-off of council houses and the encouragement of private health and education.

theodicy of disprivilege: a set of ideas used by *sect* members to justify their low socioeconomic position in that they may believe that they are 'God's chosen people' and the promise of salvation may be seen as compensation for their poverty.

■ *e.g.* Marxists are very critical of Pentecostal sects in Latin America because they transmit the message that suffering and poverty are a virtue to be welcomed and accepted as normal. Such ways of thinking promote the idea that there is no point in changing the here and now.

theory: an explanation that seeks to establish cause and effect relationships between concepts, e.g. suggesting that there is a relationship between social class and educational underachievement.

■ Sociological theory is made up of a number of different and often conflicting approaches.

third world: those countries, mainly situated in Africa, Latin America, the Indian subcontinent and East Asia, that have not achieved or are on the road to achieving development.

■ The term is now largely redundant in sociological terms because it is acknowledged that the third world is not a *homogeneous* group of countries.

■ *e.g.* Some third-world nations have rapidly industrialised in the last 30 years, i.e. the *Asian tigers*. Moreover, there is tremendous variation in development. The term *less developed countries* has become more popular among world sociologists.

thirty/thirty/forty society: the idea formulated by the economist Will Hutton that Britain has become a society split into three segments of 30%, 30% and 40% because of the demands of the free-market economy.

■ The first 30% are the disadvantaged, i.e. the unemployed and their dependants. The middle 30% is made up of marginalised and insecure workers, e.g. part-timers and casual workers. The top 40% are privileged because they are in full-time secure and regular work. Hutton's thesis is largely based on the market value of workers rather than status divisions between them and consequently he underplays gender and ethnic inequalities in the workplace.

time-budget study: the keeping of a detailed *diary* in which subjects assist researchers by observing and recording their daily lives.

■ It provides both factual and *quantitative data* in that it details the number of activities, the people involved and the social context. It also provides *qualitative data* because respondents can be asked to record their feelings about activities.

■ *e.g.* Ann Oakley's housework study asked women to record their feelings about domestic labour and childcare.

total institution: an institution in which a number of similar individuals are cut off from wider society for a length of time and follow a formally administered and strict regime in which all aspects of a person's existence are observed and regulated.

■ Examples of total institutions include psychiatric hospitals, prisons, boarding schools, army barracks, homes for the elderly, monasteries etc.

▨ *e.g.* Goffman's research into a psychiatric hospital claimed that such institutions are involved in the *mortification of self*. Some inmates may experience *institutionalisation*.

totalitarianism: the total control of a population by a single party or an individual who wields absolute power within a ruling party.

▨ All totalitarian states are dictatorships in which power is exercised using *coercion* and is not restricted by law.

trade union: organisation that aims to protect the pay, conditions and rights at work of workers.

traditional working class: see *proletarian traditionalists*.

training: the acquisition of vocational skills relevant to the workplace which until the early 1980s and the introduction of the *new vocationalism* was distinguished from academic education and carried on outside schools in the workplace.

▨ Despite the new vocationalism, there is criticism that because of the academic bias within education, qualifications that involve work experience such as *GNVQs* have not been marketed properly or have been accorded low status by teachers, universities and even some employers.

transnational company: a global business firm that has major holdings across both the *developed world* and *less developed countries* as well as across several economic areas, but with no clearly identifiable homebase.

▨ Such companies are not over-reliant on one country for the production of their goods and have generally constructed an international *division of labour* to maximise control over profits. Sociologists note that such companies have massive economic and political influence and are just as exploitative of Western economies as they are of the economies of less developed countries.

triangulation: the use of more than one method of research in order to assess the *validity* of one's research methods and especially the data produced.

▨ Usually it involves combining at least one method that produces *quantitative data* with one that produces *qualitative data*. It is a useful approach in checking on the accuracy of the data gathered by each method and also gives a more complete picture of the group being studied. The qualitative research can focus on the 'why' and 'how' of the patterns and trends of the statistics produced by the quantitative method.

▨ *TIP* Do not confuse triangulation with *methodological pluralism*.

tripartite system: a system of education resulting from the 1944 Education Act that aimed to provide three types of secondary school for different types of pupil based on an *IQ test* at the age of 11 (the *eleven-plus examination*).

▨ These schools included *grammar schools* for the most academic, secondary technical schools for the artistic and *secondary modern schools* for everyone else. All these schools were supposed to enjoy similar standards of provision, i.e. *parity of esteem*. However, few technical schools were built, the eleven-plus examination was seen to be culturally biased against working-class children and generally employers, parents and children did not see secondary moderns as having the same status as grammar schools. By the mid-1950s the over-proportionate number of middle-class pupils in grammar schools and working-class children in secondary moderns convinced social policy makers of the failure of the tripartite system and it was replaced in 1965 with the *comprehensive school*. However, vestiges of the tripartite system continue to exist today, i.e. there are approximately 130 grammar schools in England and Wales.

triple systems theory: a feminist theory of patriarchy associated with Sylvia Walby which argues that patriarchy interacts with *capitalism* and *racism* to produce gender stratification.

■ Walby argues that patriarchy is composed of three elements:

(1) Subordination — patriarchal institutions like the family, media and education inevitably produce unequal relations between men and women.

(2) Oppression — women experience sexism because men discriminate against them on the basis of unfounded stereotypes or ideology.

(3) Exploitation — men exploit women's skills and labour without rewarding them sufficiently, especially in the home.

■ *e.g.* Walby argues that this form of patriarchy results in the subordination, exploitation and oppression of women in the family, at work, in sexual relations (the sexual double standard) and in culture systems (the mass media represent women either as sex objects, appendages of men or mothers). The state also acts in the interests of men rather than women, e.g. in terms of taxation and welfare rules and the weakness of laws protecting women at work etc.

two-step flow model: an influential theory of *media effects* originating in the work of Katz and Lazarfeld that suggested that there existed powerful *opinion leaders* within audiences who were exposed to greater media content and were influential within their social circles with regard to lifestyle choices and political preferences.

■ The first step focuses on the flow of media content to opinion leaders who in the second step communicate their feelings on it to an audience. The influence of the media therefore depends on an individual's position in a set of inter-personal relationships.

underachievement: lack of educational attainment experienced particularly by pupils from working-class and ethnic minority backgrounds relative to middle-class and white pupils that is measured using a variety of indicators including literacy and numeracy abilities, membership of top and bottom streams, the number of school-leavers, qualifications such as GCSE and A-level, exclusions, and university entry and degrees.

▓ Explanations of underachievement focus on *cultural deprivation, material deprivation, classroom interaction,* the *hidden curriculum* and *cultural capital.*

▓ *TIP* Underachievement is a gender issue too. *Female underachievement* was the concern of much educational sociology in the 1970s and 1980s whilst *male underachievement* is seen as the problem today.

underclass (1): according to the *New Right,* a *dependency culture* that has appeared in the 1980s, caused by over-generous welfare benefits that allegedly act as a disincentive to work.

▓ The underclass allegedly socialises its children into deviant social values and behaviour. A large proportion of the underclass is allegedly made up of teenage mothers who lack the parental skills to control their children.

▓ *e.g.* Marsland argues that a culture of dependency has eroded the capacity of the unemployed and single mothers to be self-reliant and independent. However, there is no empirical evidence for a distinct grouping with those characteristics.

underclass (2): a social group experiencing poverty, who depend upon state benefits because of structural obstacles such as world recession, government policy, *racism* etc., which are beyond their control.

▓ This approach does not scapegoat people for their poverty.

underdevelopment: a Marxist term which suggests that the *less developed countries* have not developed to the same degree as Western countries because they have been prevented from doing so by the richer *developed world* countries.

▓ *Dependency theory,* especially as formulated by Frank, claims that there exists a global system of capitalism in which *core nations* such as the USA and UK exploit less developed countries. Frank argued that this relationship of exploitation and dependency occurred historically through slavery and *colonialism* and continues today through *neocolonialism.*

■ *TIP* Definitions of *development* are problematic and depend upon ideological position.

undeveloped country: see *less developed country*.

unemployment: the state of being without work despite being available for it.

■ Rates of unemployment are notoriously difficult to ascertain because the official way of measuring unemployment has changed 33 times since 1979. At the moment it is based upon the number of people who actually claim unemployment-related benefits. This excludes 16–17-year-olds on training schemes and anyone not eligible to claim such benefits, such as women whose partners are working, those who are unlikely to get income support, and single mothers. To claim benefit, the claimant must prove that he or she is actively seeking work. There are a range of sociological explanations for unemployment.

■ *e.g.* Market Liberals and New Right thinkers believe that too much state intervention is the cause. For example, they suggest welfare benefits are too high and this leads to less incentive to work. Marxists argue that unemployment is an inevitable feature of capitalism because new technologies introduced to boost productivity and reduce labour costs result in *deskilling* and therefore unemployment.

■ *TIP* Many sociologists are now focusing on *globalisation* as a cause of unemployment. International competition from the low-cost economies of the *less developed* and Asian tiger countries may result in transnationals closing Western factories and transferring production to the less developed world. Social problems, such as crime and delinquency and *urban riots*, may be an indirect product of unemployment. However, it is difficult to prove these links.

universalism/universalistic: a set of values used to judge individuals on *meritocratic* criteria such as examinations, qualifications, skill, ability, suitability etc.

■ Such values are seen as a key characteristic of *achievement*-orientated societies such as modern Western nations. It is argued that these values are missing in *less developed countries*, which are seen as characterised by *ascription*.

unobtrusive method: a method of research in which the subjects of the research are unaware that they are being studied.

■ *e.g. Covert participant observation* and the use of *secondary data* such as personal documents.

unstructured interview: an interview in which the interviewer informally asks *open-ended questions* about a topic and allows the respondent to respond freely and in depth.

■ Also known as a guided conversation, this method is championed by *interpretivists*, who argue that the trust generated by the informality of the interview generates more valid, *qualitative data*. Such interviews allow respondents the opportunity to say what they want rather than what the interviewer expects. *Positivists*, however, suggest that such interviews are unreliable because they are not standardised, quantifiable or replicable.

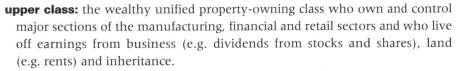

upper class: the wealthy unified property-owning class who own and control major sections of the manufacturing, financial and retail sectors and who live off earnings from business (e.g. dividends from stocks and shares), land (e.g. rents) and inheritance.

■ The top 1% of the population own about one third of all wealth in the UK. This group was considerably richer 50 years ago but has transferred a substantial part of its wealth to other family members (the top 5%), via trust funds, to avoid paying tax. The upper class (whom Marxists refer to as the *bourgeoisie* or capitalist class) practise self-recruitment, *social closure* and an influence out of all proportion to their numbers in political decision-making.

■ *TIP* The *superclass* has been identified as the latest addition to the upper class.

urbanisation: the movement of large numbers of people from rural areas to towns and cities, which became the major centres of population in the UK by the end of the nineteenth century.

urban riot: large-scale public disorder or collective protest that generally involves violence, destruction of property and confrontation with the police.

■ Riots tend to occur in working-class and ethnic minority areas with high levels of unemployment and deprivation. They may be initiated by grievances with policing strategies or, in the case of ethnic minorities, concerns about the perceived *racism* of police officers. *Left realists* blame *relative deprivation, powerlessness* and a sense of exclusion from full participation in society.

uses and gratifications theory: a theory of *media effects* that focuses on how the audience uses the media in different ways to gratify social needs such as companionship, community, escape from routine, family interaction etc.

■ This theory, associated with Blumler and McQuail, notes that different social groups have varying social needs and therefore use the media differently.

■ *e.g.* Professionals may be more interested in the cultural products associated with BBC2, whilst manual workers may access television primarily for entertainment and to escape from routine. Blumler and McQuail have been criticised for over-romanticising media content and ignoring the *dysfunctions* of the media such as 'dumbing down' and the creation of *false needs*.

validity: a genuine or true picture of the problem being studied by the sociologist, e.g. behaviour, attitudes etc.

■ When the question 'does it have validity?' is posed, it usually refers to whether the data collected give a true picture of what the sociologist is studying. It also refers to the research method adopted, because the data produced may be a product of the method used rather than a true picture of what is actually going on.

■ *e.g.* Survey-based research such as *questionnaires* and *structured interviews* are often criticised by *interpretivist* sociologists for the low *validity* of their results because it is believed there is a gap between what people say they do and what they actually do. Problems such as *interview bias or effect, yea-saying,* the *social desirability effect, demand characteristics,* artificiality and the *Hawthorne effect* also undermine validity, although some sociologists have adopted *respondent validation* to verify the validity of their findings. Interpretivists suggest methods such as *observation* and *unstructured interviews* are more likely to generate valid data because they usually take place in the natural environment of the respondents.

value: a belief and *goal* relating to what members of society feel is morally important and desirable that acts as a general guideline on standards in private and public life.

■ Values are relative to particular historical periods, societies and *subcultures.* However, some values are generally shared by most members of society, e.g. respect for human life.

■ *e.g.* Functionalists see shared values (i.e. *value consensus*) as the central component of social order in society, although Marxists suggest ideological agencies socialise members of society into bourgeois values such as respect for hierarchy and acceptance of inequality as normal and natural.

■ *TIP* Norms are values put into practice.

value consensus: a *functionalist* idea which suggests that the role of agencies such as the family, education, religion etc. is to socialise members of society into shared *norms* and *values,* which is the basis of *social order.*

■ Critical sociologists, in contrast, suggest that value consensus is a myth because the basis of social order is often either *ideology* or *coercion.*

value freedom: the *positivist* notion that facts can and ought to be separated from the values held by the researcher.

■ Weber argues that a value-free sociology was possible and developed the idea of *ideal types* in order to carry out objective sociological analysis. However, *critical sociologists* such as Marxists, feminists and *symbolic interactionists* argue that value freedom is essentially moral indifference and consequently an unethical and untenable position to take.

variable: see *dependent variable* and *independent variable*.

verstehen: the skill of being able to see the world through the eyes of the group being studied and therefore place their interpretation or understanding of the social world at the centre of the research.

■ Weber referred to this as empathetic understanding. *Interpretivists* see observation as the most effective method of obtaining verstehen, because its naturalistic approach is more likely to access the social meanings that people give to social phenomena and provide insight into the socially constructed rules that define and govern social life.

vertical extended family: see *extended family*.

vertical segregation: a type of occupational stratification by sex which allocates men and women into different levels of employment in terms of status and pay.

■ Women are more likely to be concentrated in semi-skilled and unskilled work compared with men. They are more likely to be employed in part-time work and in temporary or casual work. Even when they gain access to the professional and managerial sectors they are likely to encounter a *glass ceiling*. The average pay gap between male and female workers is approximately 18%.

■ *TIP* The most convincing sociological explanations for these gender inequalities in employment come from *feminism, dual labour market* theory and *rational choice theory*.

victimless crime: crimes that do not have any recognisable victims because both parties involved are engaged in criminal behaviour (e.g. the drug pusher and buyer, the prostitute and client).

■ Some theorists suggest that *white-collar crime* is not taken seriously by society because its nature means that there are no immediately recognisable victims — there is no 'blood on the streets' as there is with *street crime*.

victim survey: a survey such as those in the *British Crime Surveys* that asks people which crimes have been committed against them over a fixed period of time and whether or not they have been reported.

■ Such surveys tend to suggest that *official statistics* underestimate property crime. However, the BCS showed that most crime is committed against young males in inner-city areas rather than older people or females, although the Islington Crime Survey suggested that women were more at risk in the inner city. Most importantly, victim surveys seem to suggest that current policing policy has little impact on the crime rate.

■ *TIP* There are methodological problems inherent in this approach in that certain social groups and certain crimes are omitted from the research process and such surveys are heavily dependent on crimes that people are aware have been committed against them.

wealth: refers to assets such as capital, property and land, stocks and shares, antiques, paintings, jewellery etc. held by individuals or social groups that are surplus to everyday requirements in terms of standard of living.

■ Although there has been a gradual redistribution of wealth in the UK, it has been very narrow, i.e. from the very wealthy (the top 1%) to the wealthy (the top 10%) in order to avoid death duties. Inheritance is still an important source of wealth. The amount of wealth in the hands of the top 10% is probably an underestimate. It is difficult to acquire accurate data on wealth because of tax avoidance schemes, overseas investments etc.

welfare dependency: an idea associated with the *New Right* and particularly their definition of the *underclass* which states that certain groups in the population have become over-reliant on easily obtainable and over-generous state benefits, which has undermined their ability to look after themselves.

■ It is often contrasted with the social democratic approach to welfare, which claims that the organisation of the *welfare state* contributes to poverty because of the *poverty trap* and because benefits are too low.

welfare pluralism: the idea that the state should provide welfare services in conjunction with other agencies such as the voluntary sector, i.e. charities, and the formal sector, i.e. families, and the *private sector*, i.e. private pensions, education and health schemes.

■ The *welfare state* in the UK has generally been characterised by welfare pluralism, although *care in the community* increased the role of agencies like the family in taking greater responsibility, especially for the elderly, disabled and mentally ill.

welfare state: a system of government that takes responsibility for the welfare of people by providing a range of benefits including free education and health care, council housing and support in times of need such as sickness, disability, old age and unemployment.

■ The commitment of the state to its citizens is seen to extend from the 'cradle to the grave'.

■ *e.g.* Beveridge, seen by many as the founder of the modern welfare state, aimed to eradicate the five giant evils of want, idleness, ignorance, squalor and disease.

W

Between 1950 and 1979 there was a consensus with regard to how the Labour and Conservative governments saw the welfare state. However, concerns about the rising costs of welfare and welfare dependency led to Thatcher's government introducing more *selective benefits* and *means-tested benefits*, privatising some services (e.g. selling off council houses), reducing some benefits and introducing *care in the community*.

welfare to work: a New Labour policy, part of the 'New Deal', which aims to reduce poverty and welfare costs by encouraging lone parents, the unemployed and the long-term sick and disabled to overcome the 'poverty of ambition', i.e. *welfare dependency*, by enabling them to find jobs.

■ There is an element of compulsion in this policy, in that failure to attend job interviews results in the cutting off of benefits. With regard to single mothers, this policy has resulted in training and help with childcare costs to get them into employment.

■ *TIP* Note that the idea of welfare dependency and therefore the implication that an *underclass* exists is not solely the view of the *New Right*.

West Indian: see *African-Caribbean*.

white-collar crime: a catch-all term used to describe crimes committed in the course of legitimate employment that involve the abuse of power and trust including fraud, false accounting, tax evasion, computer fraud, insider dealing etc.

■ Some sociologists prefer to distinguish between 'occupational crime', committed by lower-level employees and senior executives, *corporate crime*, committed by large corporations (e.g. pollution, non-compliance to health and safety legislation, resulting in death or injury to workers, consumers or passengers), and *organisational crime*, committed by public organisations or the government. Sociologists point out that white-collar crime, despite its financial cost, is rarely taken seriously by the general public for a number of reasons. Such crimes are seldom visible, they are complex and morally ambiguous (e.g. tax evasion is rarely seen as 'wrong') and, moreover, they are often dealt with 'off the record' if detected, because the police do not have the resources to prosecute such crime.

white-collar workers: traditionally all *non-manual workers*, including management and professionals who were classified as middle-class, but which is now increasingly used to describe clerical workers, secretaries, call-centre workers etc.

■ It has been suggested by the Marxist Harry Braverman that clerical workers have been *deskilled* and have subsequently experienced *proletarianisation*.

work: in capitalist societies work tends to be described as waged labour that takes place within a formal economy and which confers *identity* and *status* on workers.

■ The supremacy of wage labour often means that there are negative consequences for the unemployed and the retired in terms of loss of status and identity. Feminists note that *domestic labour* is rarely defined as real work because it is unpaid. *Marxists* argue that work should be a creative, fulfilling activity but in capitalist societies it has become a commodity to be sold, exploited, *deskilled* and controlled by management, resulting in the *alienation* of workers — a means to an end rather than an end in itself.

■ *TIP* The debate between Marxists and Robert Blauner is about the nature of work in capitalist societies.

working class: a social class made up of those who earn wages through manual labour.

■ This class is sometimes referred to as *blue-collar workers*. Some sociologists have pointed to the existence of distinct subcultural groups existing within the working class: the *proletarian traditionalists, deferential workers, instrumental collectivists*, the *underclass* etc. Marxists, who refer to the working class as the *proletariat*, suggest that some traditionally middle-class occupations such as *white-collar work* are undergoing *proletarianisation* and are now working-class.

working mother: a mother with young children who goes out to work. Such women are often scapegoated by the media, politicians and *moral entrepreneurs* for neglecting their children and causing social problems such as youth crime.

■ This idea was very influenced by the psychologist John Bowlby's ideas on maternal deprivation. However, there is little empirical evidence to support the idea that working mothers 'damage' their children.

■ *e.g.* Studies suggest that children require consistent parenting rather than mothering. Feminists suggest that the ideology of maternal deprivation is a product of *patriarchy*, which seeks to justify men's dominance of the labour market.

work satisfaction: the pleasure associated with the idea of work being an end in itself because it allows the possibility of self-expression, creativity and fulfilment.

■ Marxists argue that the organisation of capitalist production has reduced the possibility of work offering such possibilities to the working class and some sections of the middle class. Blauner argues that work satisfaction and *alienation* depend on the technology present in particular industries.

world-accommodating sect: part of Wallis' typology of *new religious movements*, such religions neither fully accept the values and goals of wider society nor entirely reject society.

■ Wallis notes that the *new evangelical movement*, made up of *fundamentalist* 'born-again' Christians, exists on the margins of the established church and *denominations*, which is typical of a world-accommodating sect.

world-affirming sect: part of Wallis' typology of *new religious movements*, such religions accept the values and goals of wider society but aim to provide a new means to achieve them.

■ Human beings are seen as having enormous physical and mental potential and these sects advertise themselves as being able effectively to tap into this, usually for a fee, so that people can achieve economic and social fulfilment.

W

■ *e.g.* Scientology fits the characteristics of this sort of sect.

world-rejecting sect: part of Wallis' typology of *new religious movements*, such religions see the secular world as a corrupt place and consequently either cut themselves off from society or attempt to do battle with *secularisation* through evangelism and conversion.

■ Such sects tend to demand a great deal of commitment from their members, e.g. the cutting off of friends and relations, adoption of an ascetic lifestyle and sometimes even self-sacrifice in the form of suicide.

world sociology: the sociological study of the relationship between different countries of the world.

■ It especially focuses on the economic inequalities between the developed industrialised West and the less-developed world of Africa, Asia and Central and South America.

world system theory: a theory, associated with Wallerstein, which suggests that the modern world system is characterised by one world economy (i.e. capitalism).

■ In this system *core nations* (i.e. capitalist countries like Great Britain) interact with semi-periphery countries (i.e. countries like the *Asian tigers* on their way to full development) and periphery countries (i.e. those whose economies still revolve around the export of cash crops and raw materials). This theory is flexible in that it can explain the changes in the fortunes of the individual nations as some countries sometimes move up or down the world hierarchy.

xenophobia: an exaggerated fear or loathing towards foreigners, expressed through *prejudice* and *discrimination*.

yea-saying: a type of subject effect associated with *questionnaires* and *structured interviews* which may affect both the reliability of the research method and the validity of the data collected.
- Pawson notes that because people are so 'nice', they prefer on balance to acquiesce.
- *e.g.* Attitude surveys using questions asking respondents to 'agree' or 'disagree' or be 'satisfied' or 'unsatisfied' may find some bias in favour of the positive response which may not reflect the reality of people's lives.

youth culture: the features of a *subculture*, such as style of dress, music, speech and behaviour, seen as specific to young people.
- Sociologists have looked at youth culture in two broad ways. First, it is doubtful that one youth culture exists, with a set of norms, values and attitudes shared by all young people that diverges from that of the adult generation. Surveys consistently show that the majority of youth are conformist and generally share the attitudes of their parents. Second, sociologists have focused on deviant youth subcultures such as teddy boys, mods, rockers, skinheads and punks. For example, Marxists have tended to explain the behaviour of the minority who participate in these cultures as a form of working-class *resistance* to *bourgeois hegemony* and a means of magically reclaiming working-class community under threat from unemployment and the declining inner city. Others, e.g. Stan Cohen, claim such youth subcultures are often the creation of the mass media.

youth training scheme: see *new vocationalism*.

zero tolerance: a form of *policing* inspired by the theory of 'broken windows' that reverses the previous policing policy of only giving priority to serious crimes and which insists that the police should crack down on petty crime and disorderly behaviour.
- It was first put into operation in New York city in 1993–94 and resulted in a significant drop in the crime rate, especially homicide, which fell by 50%.

Several police forces in the UK have adopted similar methods, although opinions regarding the success of this policy are mixed.

zone of transition: the inner zone of large cities that is characterised in periods of growth by a transitory population, a lack of *community* and consequently weak social controls, which lead to high crime rates.

■ This theory originated with Shaw and Mckay who suggested that the disequilibrium and chaos that characterised such areas caused crime. This *pathological* theory has been criticised for being a circular argument, i.e. because an area is seen to have high crime it is assumed to be disorganised, which allegedly accounts for the crime. It is not clear which is the *independent variable* — the disorganisation or the crime.